Quantrill's Raiders in Texas

Evault Boswell

EAKIN PRESS ⬧ Fort Worth, Texas

Library of Congress Cataloging-in-Publication Data

Boswell, Evault.
  Quantrill's raiders in Texas / by Evault Boswell.– 1st ed.
    p.   cm.
  Includes bibliographical references (p.) and index.
    ISBN 1-57168-784-X
    1. Quantrill, William Clarke, 1837-1865. 2. Texas–History–Civil War,
  1861-1865–Commando operations. 3. United States–History–Civil War,
  1861-1865–Commando operations. 4. Texas–History–Civil War, 1861-
  1865–Underground movements. 5. United States–History–Civil War,
  1861-1865–Underground movements. 6. Guerrillas–Texas–History–19th
  century. 7. Guerrillas–Confederate States of America–Biography. 8.
  Soldiers–Confederate States of America–Biography. 9. Sherman
  (Tex.)–History–19th century. I. Title
  E470.45.B675   2003
  973.7'42–dc21   2003000273

CONTENTS

PREFACE

In his book *Texas, the Dark Corner of the Confederacy,* B. P. Gallaway, professor of history at Abilene Christian University, deemed it necessary to include an appendix entitled: "An Essay on Texas Civil War Historiography," written by Professor Alwyn Barr when he was a research associate with the Texas State Historical Society. Eighteen pages were devoted to summarizing all that has been written about the Civil War in Texas. But there is still much to be said, and probably even more to be discovered, about the conflict that shattered the history of the young state of Texas and splintered its inhabitants.

Many thousands of words have also been written about the guerrilla William Clarke Quantrill, from William Connelley's biased *Quantrill and the Border Wars,* written in 1910, to *The Devil Knows How to Ride,* by Edward E. Leslie, published in 1996, which may be the most comprehensive work done on Quantrill's life.

Sandwiched in between those volumes is *William Clarke Quantrill: His Life and Times,* by Albert Castel, published in 1962. Castel was a professor of American history at Western Michigan University. Add to the list Carl Breihan's *Quantrill and His Civil War Guerrillas,* published in 1959. Breihan and Castel are the most prolific writers on the guerrilla war in Missouri. Another recent publication is *Quantrill's War: The Life and Times of William Clarke Quantrill,* written by Duane Schultz and published in 1996 by St. Martin's Press.

Other books on the subject include *Gray Ghosts of the Confederacy,* by Richard S. Brownlee, and *Bloody Bill Anderson,* by Castel and Thomas Goodrich. Michael Fellman's *Inside War* is an excellent account of the guerrilla conflict in Missouri, and Jay Monaghan's *Civil War on the Western Border, 1854–1865,* gives a good account of the events that led to the conflict. Thomas Goodrich wrote *Black Flag* in 1995, which is another good book on the Civil War in Missouri.

For insight into the way of life experienced by the citizens of Missouri during the war, *Missouri Ordeal, 1862–1864: Diaries of Willard Hall Mendenhall* is a must-read. Mendenhall lived in Lexington, and these dairies of a Northern sympathizer, living in the belly of Southern rebellion, record how his family survived.

Contemporary writers of Quantrill had limited written material to call upon and thus relied on the testimonies of the men who rode with Quantrill; as in the case of *Three Years with Quantrill* by John McCorkle, these accounts were generally biased. The same is true of *Charles W. Quantrell; A True History of His Guerrilla Welfare,* as told by Captain Harrison Trow to J. P. Burch and copyrighted in 1923. William Gregg's *A Little Dab of History without Embellishment,* which was never published but is at the Missouri State Historical Society in Columbia, is hardly trustworthy but does offer insight into the guerrilla lifestyle not found in other manuscripts.

So much has been written about Jesse and Frank James that it is difficult to separate fact from fiction. One of the most noted, which was on the borderline between fact and imagination, is Frank Triplett's *The Life, Times, and Treacherous Death of Jesse James*. In Breihan's book, *Complete and Authentic Life of Jesse James,* a great many words were written to prove that J. Dalton was not Jesse, and much of the book focused on the banditry after the war, with very little about Jesse's participation with Quantrill's guerrillas.

Pulp fiction writers and Hollywood have so distorted the life and times of the James brothers that it may be impossible to ferret out the truth.

Probably no book had more effect on the public and historical image of the guerrillas than *Noted Guerrillas,* written in 1877 by Newman Edwards, who served on the staff of General Jo Shelby during the war.

Edwards' glamorous prose as a journalist after the war created the Robin Hood personification of Jesse James that is still accepted by many today. Edwards' description of the guerrilla transformed the ragged, dirty, teenage farm boys into saints, even if their halos are a bit tainted with the blood of innocent victims:

> They had passwords that only the initiated understood, and signals which meant everything or nothing. A night bird was a messenger; a day bird a courier. . . . They knew the names or the numbers of the pursuing regiments from the shoes of their horses, and told the nationality of troops by the manner in which twigs were broken along the line of march. They could see in the night like other beasts of prey, and hunted most when it was darkest. No matter for a road so only there was a trail, and no matter for a trail so only there was a direction. When there was no wind, and when the clouds hid the sun or the stars, they traveled by the moss on the trees. In the day time they looked for this moss with their eyes, in the night time with their hands. Living much in fastnesses, [*sic*] they were rarely surprised, while solitude developed and made more acute the every instinct of self-preservation. By degrees a caste began to be established. . . . Free to come and go; bound by no enlistment and dependent upon no bounty; hunted by one nation and apologized for by the other; merciful rarely and merciless often; loving liberty in a blind, idolatrous fashion, half reality and half superstition; holding no crime as bad as that of cowardice; courteous to women amid all the wild license of pillage and slaughter; steadfast as faith to comradeship or friend; too serious for boastfulness and too near the unknown to deceive themselves with vanity.

It is true that most of the bushwhackers were excellent woodsmen, riders, and shooters. They were also "steadfast as faith to comradeship or friend"—except when they were drunk or there was loot to be divided.

All of these books were written after the fact, and time may have dimmed the vision and memory of those who actually rode with the bushwhackers; and in some cases, the events seem to have been recalled as the writer may have wished them to be, not as they were.

For instance, McCorkle remembered Christmas week of 1863 as a time of great fun, with the young people of Sherman, Texas, inviting the guerrillas into town for a ball and later extending an invitation to visit Brig. Gen. Henry McCulloch at Bonham.

The "ball" actually took place on New Year's, and the young people of Sherman who invited the marauders were the saloon girls at Jim Crow Chile's saloon and gambling den. The invitation to Bonham was a trap set up by McCulloch that ended in the arrest and escape of Quantrill and the beginning of the end of his command.

McCorkle wrote his book *Three Years with Quantrill* in 1892, almost thirty years after the fact, and his memory was probably unreliable, for he reported that the collapse of the jail in Kansas City, which killed and wounded several of the bushwhackers' women, took place after the raiders' sojourn in Texas.

McCorkle also recalled the marriage of one of the bushwhackers to a young lady of Sherman. The bushwhacker was Bill Anderson (who had yet to earn the nickname "Bloody") and the woman was Bush Smith, supposedly one of the "working girls" from Chile's saloon.

Several writers seemed to doubt whether Anderson and Smith were ever really married, but a copy of their marriage certificate, duly signed by S. Bostick, clerk of Grayson County Court, on March 2, 1863, was found recorded at the courthouse in Sherman,Texas. Some have suggested that the name "Bush" had sexual connotations, but it was actually a family name, perhaps her mother's maiden name. Her first name is illegible on the marriage certificate but was perhaps "Adel" or "Adeline." She was also a member of the Methodist Church, which casts doubt on the idea proposed by most historians that she was a prostitute.

Anderson could have had her favors without marriage if she had been a loose woman. So why would he marry her? When he was killed, a love note from her and locks of her hair were found among his possessions. He also bought her a home in Sherman before he went back to Missouri, evidently planning on returning.

Connelley's view of the guerrillas was based on a strong affection for the North, and he had an eagerness to accept the Federal point of view. He did interview a great many of the actual participants after they had grown old, but as J. C. Blake of Longview said in his memoirs, written in 1912; "My age is 72 years and time has caused me to forget much." [1]

Connelley spent much time on extensive footnotes explaining his opinion and relied heavily on the letters of W. L. Potter, written to W. W. Scott, a Quantrill family friend from Canal Dover, Ohio, who dug up Quantrill's bones and sold them. Hardly a reliable source for information, but he does add pieces to the puzzle.

It is also interesting to note that Breihan did not even include Potter as one of Quantrill's men in *Quantrill and His Civil War Guerrillas*. Connelley listed Potter as a "hanger-on" who boasted of being close to Quantrill but discounted his reports almost entirely.

During the war, many of Quantrill's men were very young; some, like Jesse James and Allen Parmer, were only teenagers. Many of them were illiterate, and even for those who did know how to write, keeping a diary or record of events was difficult considering their lifestyle. Unlike other facets of the Civil War, such as the major battles of the East and the generals who fought them, very little primary material exists about the guerrillas on the western edge of the conflict. And so, many memoirs were written years after the conflict had ceased. In the case of most veterans, time also caused them to remember much, and perhaps some of their reminiscences grew with each telling.

But this is not just a book about Quantrill and his guerrillas, or a book about Texas in the Civil War, but rather a recounting of the events that led up to the impact of the famed guerrilla and his cutthroats on Northeast Texas, primarily Grayson County and the city of Sherman, and particularly during the winter of 1863.

It is also a review of the events that led to the conditions in northeast Texas before the war. The events preceding the war had an astounding impact on the guerrillas' actions while in

Texas, the response of the citizens of Sherman to those actions, and even the aftermath of the war.

The thesis of the book, as far as Quantrill and his men are concerned, is to show the sequence of events, from the no-quarter-given ruling, or the black flag, which stated that guerrillas would be killed when captured, and its enforcement by Gen. James Blunt; to the collapse of the jail in Kansas City, which killed some of the wives and sisters of the bushwhackers; to the rape of Lawrence, Kansas, the culmination of Quantrill's hatred; to Order No. 11 by Thomas Ewing, which forced the evacuation of all Southern sympathizers from certain counties of Missouri on the western border and helped drive the bushwhackers to Texas.[2]

Most of the raiders, when interviewed later in life, reported that the reason they participated at Lawrence was to avenge the deaths of their wives and daughters in the jail collapse in Kansas City, even if they had no relatives imprisoned there.

Make no mistake, most of the guerrillas had justifiable cause to hate Yankees and Jayhawkers. The atrocities reportedly committed by the guerrillas were, at least to some extent, just an amplified reflection of the violations of human rights by Jayhawkers and Union soldiers.

But Quantrill's purpose for the Lawrence raid was purely personal. He had been treated badly there before the war for petty crimes and yearned for revenge. William Gregg, his first lieutenant, who rode with Quantrill from almost the very beginning and survived the war as a member of the regular Confederate army, said of Quantrill: "He longed to get even with Kansas. His proposition was to go to Lawrence." He called Lawrence a "great hot-bed of abolitionism in Kansas" and added, "We can get more revenge and more money there than anywhere else in the State of Kansas."[3]

Quantrill stated later in a letter by C. M. Chase, a writer for the *True Republican and Sentinel* at Sycamore, Illinois, that "he was surprised that his men were murdering people, but said they had got into the saloons, got drunk and beyond his control. He came to destroy the town and plunder its wealth, in retaliation for Lane burning Osceola." Connelley severely questioned this report by Chase.

✖

Thomas Goodrich, in his book *Bloody Dawn,* softened the image of Quantrill. Goodrich even suggested that one of the reasons Quantrill did not make another raid such as Lawrence was the "likelihood that Quantrill, the refined schoolteacher, had no stomach for the brutal savagery that later shamed the fighting in Missouri and the ugly games played with fervor by both sides."[4]

Tell that to the mother of the twelve-year-old drummer boy who was burned to death at Baxter Springs.

Some have claimed that the sacking of Lawrence was ordered by Gen. Sterling Price in retaliation for the destruction of his stores at Osceola, but Connelley, normally in accord with the Northern side of any question, repudiated this charge, stating that "General Price was a humane man and an honorable soldier, and it is not probable that he advised any such course."

In defense of the guerrillas, it must be said that tremendous atrocities were carried out against innocent families in Missouri, even some who did not espouse the Southern cause.

It began with the Jayhawkers and the Redlegs, certainly not to be mistaken for Federal troops, who butchered and robbed families along the western border of the state. Lawrence was the home of Kansas senator James Lane, at that time the man the guerrillas hated the most, who escaped the carnage.

With the advent of the war, many vigilante groups, made up mostly of citizens with personal vendettas, terrorized local enemies who were even suspected of being pro-Southern and many who were completely neutral.

Then, as the war began, the Union troops who flooded into the state, many of them of German descent, added to the misery of the honest and not-so-honest citizens of Missouri.

In a letter from J.T.K. Hayward to J. W. Brooks, dated August 13, 1861, it was pointed out that the Federal troops were helping themselves to fill their needs:

> . . . there is added to this the irregularities of the soldiery, such as taking poultry, pigs, milk, butter, preserves, potatoes, horses, and in fact everything they want; entering and searching houses, and stealing in many cases; committing rapes on the negroes and such like things—the effect has been to make

a great many Union men inveterate enemies, and if these things continue much longer, our cause is ruined. These things are not exaggerated by me, and, though they do not characterize all the troops, several regiments have conducted in this way, and have repeatedly fired on peaceable citizens—sometimes from trains as they passed—and no punishment, or none of any account has been meted out to them. Then, drunkenness is a great curse of officers and men.[5]

But it would seem the Federal troops were carrying out the orders issued by none other than U. S. Grant, brigadier general: "When it is necessary to get provisions for your men, you will take them from active secessionists, if practicable; if not practicable, from Union or law-abiding citizens, giving an order on the post commissary here for the pay. Compel persons whose teams you press to send teamsters to take the teams back. You have my private instructions how to conduct this pressing business so as to make it as little offensive as possible."

Pressing horses and mules became a lucrative business for some of the Federal officers, who shipped them to Quincy, Illinois, to be sold and the funds placed in their personal accounts. One regiment was also accused of stealing slaves. Law-abiding citizens across the northern tier of the state were informed that they would be responsible for—and required to pay for—railroads and communications lines destroyed by rebels in their area.

Probably no event in the war, however, was more pivotal in turning the guerrillas into killers and mutilators than the collapse of the so-called jail in Kansas City that killed and maimed some of their women. They were convinced that it was a deliberate act by the Federals.

The black-flag order, which gave guerrillas no hope of survival if captured, led to their own practice of not taking prisoners, at least not for very long.

All of these events, falling like dominoes stood on end, culminated in the withdrawal of the bushwhackers toward Texas and led to the massacre of General Blunt's band at Baxter Springs and the ultimate breakup of the Quantrill gang in Texas.

In an effort to re-create the times, this book is written in three parts. The first deals with the historical events and characters, both civilian and military, Missourians and Texans, that marked the final days of the Quantrill guerrillas in Texas in 1863.

There is also a biographical sketch of each of the prime players in the drama that unfolded in Grayson County. In the first part of the book, the characters are described along with the events that led up to their participation in the history of Texas. In the second part, a review is made of what happened to each of them after the episode that changed so many lives in Texas.

It is impossible to re-create the thinking of the participants, for the events took place in an era when social and moral standards varied from the very formal and moral, to the extremely decadent and amoral.

Applying today's morality and social graces to a particular historical time or event is not only difficult but unnecessary. Looking at people as they were and seeing them react to events and circumstances is part of the historian's task.

Regardless of the brutality shown by the guerrillas and the animalistic treatment of some innocents, it is well to remember that the Union soldiers and the Kansas Jayhawkers inflicted uncivilized acts upon the families of some of the bushwhackers. Even the abolitionist John Brown, along with his sons, chopped some victims into pieces in the name of God.

The war in Kansas and Missouri was not a struggle between good and evil. There were no good guys, only bad. History has been distorted to some extent by zealotry and wishful thinking. Preserving the truth is not always simple, but trying to change history to conform to modern-day thinking is unnecessary if we are to see the events and the personalities as they really were, not as we would have them be.

Having been raised in Missouri, there was never any doubt in my mind that Jesse James was a folk hero, the very epitome of righteousness, valor, and chivalry. And Jesse did possess, at least to some extent, all of those qualities, but like most of his comrades in arms, he also had a dark side.

The second part of this book is written to record the events that took place in Texas, particularly in Grayson County, that affected the lives of the citizens and the history of the area.

To understand the conflict that took place, not only between the guerrillas themselves but between the citizens of Grayson County and the raiders, you must catch a glimpse of the sophistication of the society into which the rough farm boys from Missouri had been cast.

North Texas was a hodgepodge of migrants from the border states, who had moved there to escape the war, and a few large plantation owners who had transferred their operations to North Texas to avoid the coming fury. And there were even a few pioneer families, such as Sophia and Maj. George Butt.

Part three relates the aftermath of the events and the end, or new beginning, for the guerrillas and the others who played a part in Grayson County's claim to history during the Civil War.

It was a time when brother fought against brother. Particularly in the northern tier of Texas counties bordering on the Red River, the division was so strong that the people of Gainesville hanged forty-two of their fellow citizens because of rumors of an uprising of the Federal sympathizers in the area.[6]

At the same time, hundreds of men hid out in the brush of Jernigan Thicket to avoid fighting for either side.

It was also a time of great social events, and the parties thrown at the Potts Plantation and Sophia Butt's Glen Eden were legendary. Telling the story of northeast Texas during the war is impossible without relating the stories of the citizens of Grayson County who were affected, either positively or negatively, by the rough, brash, and dirty bushwhackers from Missouri and their charismatic, sadistic, and brilliant leader, William Clarke Quantrill.

PART I

William Clarke Quantrill

CHAPTER 1

Texas Before the War

William Clarke Quantrill thought he owned a piece of Texas. Whether it was fact or fiction, the family history implied that a relative, perhaps an uncle of Quantrill's, had fought for Texas in the war with Mexico, and veterans of that war were indeed granted a tract of land. Quantrill sometimes used the alias Charley Hart, a name well known in northeast Texas, for John Hart was the first English-speaking pioneer in the area and his son, Harden Hart, served as a district judge during Reconstruction times. There was also Martin Hart, who raised his own company of Yankee sympathizers in Greenville, Texas, and headed north, supposedly to join the regular Union army, but only got as far as Arkansas, where he fought in guerrilla fashion and was hanged.

If Quantrill was kin to the Harts of north Texas, he was fighting on the wrong side, for most of them were Union to the bone. In his memoirs, Capt. J. E. Carraway did mention a "Morge" Hart, who rode with Bedford Forest but was assassinated when he got home from the war.

On September 18, 1855, Quantrill wrote his mother:

Dear Mother:
    I received your letter yesterday & was very glad to hear that you are well & I am glad to tell you that I am the same. Well I

guess I will teach school this winter, but I was very sorry to hear that you could not find those Texas papers but I want you to look again for them for if you find them I can make some money this winter.

Caroline Cornelia Clarke Quantrill, in her union with Thomas Henry Quantrill, had many heartaches, including the deaths of four of her eight children in infancy.

She must have found little comfort in the letters from her oldest (in spite of his later claims to the contrary), who wrote her to send money to help with the family but never seemed to get around to doing it.

In 1890, her only remaining son wrote her from Burnet, Texas, and, like his brother William, promised he would soon have money and succeed in Texas, where his brother had failed:

> Burnet, Texas, Feb 17, 1890
> Mrs. Caroline Quantrell
> Dear Mother
>   i Take The Pleasure of Droping you a few Lines To Let you know That i am Well and hope you are Well also i Think of you day and night and Will Send for you in The Spring I have Left that Part of The Country i Was in and am going To The Capital i think i Can Catch on to Something There The Peopel is Verry kind to me We have PLenty of friends out here Every Body is Shaking hant With me i have to Do Something Before Spring Dit You Receive my Last Letter Dont Worry aBout me i Will try and have Money By Spring Texas is my State to Live in it is a fine CLimate Would You Like to Live on The Cost The Peopel say i Look Brave Like William most all of The Young Ladies fall in Love With me BeCause They say i am so hansome i Was at a Big Gathering Lately and We had a Big time They Preachiate us highly and Wold Like verry much to see you i have Somethin in View i may make it if so i Will have PLenty of money if i Win i Will Clise for the Preasant Right soon and tell me all The News i Will Right more the Next time give my RespeCts to The friends if There is any.
>   Yours as Ever and affectinate Son
>   Thomas Quantrell address at austin Transit Co. Texas.

The letter must have reminded Caroline of the ones she had received from William thirty years earlier, except for the fact that Bill was more educated than Thomas.

As he was to prove in later years, William Clarke had concern only for his own well-being, and his letter to urge his mother to find the papers was strictly for self-indulgence. It is doubtful that Quantrill had any desire to be a farmer or rancher, so his plan must have been to sell the land, if his mother could only find the papers.

In other correspondence with his mother, he urged her to sell her home in Dover so he could buy a farm in Kansas and claimed he had sent her money on two occasions, although she did not receive it.

The several trips he made to Texas before 1863 were probably efforts to obtain some sort of documentation or testimony that would prove his claim to land in the Lone Star State.

On one such trip in 1861 with a friend who was moving his slaves to Texas, Quantrill crossed over into Indian Territory and rode with a half-breed Cherokee, Joel Mayes, who was a Confederate. Quantrill rode with the Indian raiders and must have learned a number of tricks that were to benefit him later as a bushwhacker. But Mayes joined McCulloch in the regular Confederate forces, and Quantrill wanted no part of that.

According to Connelley, they were reunited at the Battle of Wilson's Creek, Quantrill's one and only real battle, but since Mayes and his Cherokees were riding with McCulloch, Quantrill deserted him to follow Sterling Price, apparently because he wanted to stay in Missouri with a mistress named Anna.

Quantrill's trips to Texas, including a short one in 1862, did not qualify him to be called pilgrim, pioneer, or immigrant.

Efforts to entice immigrants to Texas used as bait large chunks of land, for example, the law that provided 1,280 acres to a family man who moved into Texas between March of 1836 and October of 1837. This award was later lowered to 640 acres. Earlier grants of as much as 4,000 acres had ceased when most of the "immigrants" immediately sold off most of their land because it was too much for a man to farm. Later grants stipulated that the owner must occupy the land for a minimum of three years.

The flow of settlers into Texas blossomed unabated as thousands crossed the Red or Sabine rivers. The reasons for coming to Texas varied from economic to political. Early pioneers were motivated by the promise of free land and an escape from economic depression.

Migration patterns show that most of the pilgrims came from the upper South, primarily from Missouri, Arkansas, and Tennessee, but as the Civil War approached, great numbers began to move to Texas from the lower southern states, crossing Louisiana to reach the promised land.[1]

The victory at San Jacinto increased the migration, and with a powerful foe just south of the Rio Grande still a threat to life and property, a lot of the pilgrims stayed in the northern tier of the state.

The vast, fertile soil of northeast Texas caught the eye of many a plantation owner, and because slavery was endangered, the new territory became a haven for plantation owners and their chattel.

In 1850, Texas had 154,034 whites, 397 black freedmen, and 58,161 slaves. By 1860, the population had grown to 604,215 and there were 182,000 slaves, and most of these were in the northern part of the state, since the slaves in southern cities were mostly household servants.

In 1850, Grayson County had 1,822 white residents and 186 slaves, but by 1860, the population had grown to 6,892 while the slaves increased in number to 1,292, or 15.8 percent of the total, compared to only 9.3 percent in 1850.

When half-breed Chickasaw Indian Benjamin Franklin Colbert, with the help of Joseph W. Earhart, established a ferry across the Red River just above Sherman, Texas, in 1847, he could not have foreseen what a role his commercial endeavor would play in the history of northeast Texas in the years ahead.

Perhaps he was inspired by the success of the ferry across the Sabine, over which flowed 3,000 immigrants in 1836, driven by the continuing depression and crop failures in the United States.

Pilgrims were willing to load their sparse belongings onto a wagon pulled by oxen or mules, or lash what little they owned to a raft and make the treacherous journey across Indian country regardless of the risks.

In 1843, Republic of Texas President Sam Houston, despairing of negotiations for annexation with the United States, sent a minister to Washington with the message that his nation was no longer interested in joining the Union.

However, negotiations were reopened to consider annexation in spite of a warning from Mexico that it could result in war. It did, indeed, result in war, and many of the officers of the United States who fought side by side to win the victory would in a few short years divide into separate armies and fight each other.

The question of bringing Texas into the Union as a free state held little sway, and for all practical purposes, it already was a slave state.

In March 1843, John Quincy Adams and twelve members of the House of Representatives warned of a conspiracy on the part of the South to bring Texas into the Union as a slave state. A treaty was signed on April 12, 1844, providing for Texas to be annexed as a territory. John Caldwell Calhoun explained that the treaty was "made necessary in order to preserve domestic institutions, placed under the guaranty of the Constitutions of the United States and Texas." There was also an attempt to divide Texas into six separate states.

But the political maneuvering and the pro-slavery and anti-slavery factions could not stem the flow of honest settlers and even many undesirable citizens to the great wide-open spaces of Texas.

Most of the earlier immigrants were of solid stock, merely looking for a new life. That was to change to some extent when the Civil began. Directly to the north, in Kansas and Missouri, events were taking place that would force many to made the trek to Texas. Again, it was the battle between the abolitionists of Kansas and the pro-slavery factions of Missouri that began to make life in these states, particularly on the border, not only intolerable but sometimes fatal.

Border ruffians began to spread their venom of death across the border between the two states, and whether they were called Jayhawkers, Redlegs, guerrillas, or bushwhackers, there was no middle ground to stand on. Many citizens, reading the handwriting on the wall of worse things to come, packed up their sparse belongings and their children and headed for Utah or Texas through still-dangerous Indian Territory.

There were also those pioneers who had another reason to move to Texas: to vote on the matter of secession from the Union.

In April of 1861, James Bourland, James Harrison, and Charles Hamilton, commissioned to meet with the Indians north of the Red River to ascertain whether they were pro-South or pro-North, found the Choctaws and Chickasaws to be "entirely Southern and determined to adhere to the fortunes of the South."[2]

On their return trip, the commissioners met 120 wagons filled with pilgrims in reverse. Without revealing their identities, the Texans learned that the travelers were from Grayson, Johnson, Collin, and Denton counties and were returning to Kansas after failing to sway the vote against secession, and they told Bourland they had even campaigned for the northern tier of counties to form a new state. Bourland reported that, having failed in that effort, about 500 voters were returning from whence they had come.

Fanatic abolitionist John Brown, who chopped some of his victims into pieces in the name of God, spread his gospel of death in Kansas before he took it to Harper's Ferry in an attempt to start a slave uprising. He was defeated by Robert E. Lee, and at his hanging, Thomas (not yet Stonewall) Jackson was in command of the VMI cadets who attended. They would soon join forces to protect the very institution of slavery that Brown tried to destroy. In spite of their differences, the ultra-religious Jackson offered up a prayer for the salvation of John Brown as he rode to his gallows sitting on top of his black walnut coffin: "I was much impressed with the thought that before me stood a man in the full vigor of health, who must in a few moments enter eternity. I sent up a petition that he might be saved, for awful was the thought that he might in a few minutes receive the sentence, 'Depart ye wicked, into everlasting fire.' I hope he was prepared to die, but I am doubtful."[3]

The battle for Kansas between abolitionists and pro-slavery forces is said by some to be the true beginning of the Civil War, and a great part of the conflict was moving south, to Texas.

Melinda Rankin was a Presbyterian missionary determined

to take the Gospel to Old Mexico but was forced to remain in Texas because of the lack of religious freedom in Mexico. She decided to make the most of it and opened a school in Brownsville. She had puritan ideals and great expectations for Texas. In 1850 she wrote: "An influx of intelligent and enterprising citizens has given such an additional strength that the year of improvement is fast advancing; and should it continue to be propelled with the acceleration velocity which may be reasonably expected, Texas is destined to be, ere many years, a state, which, in importance, will be second to none other in the Union."

Miss Rankin apparently looked through rose-colored glasses as the immigrant wagons and trains became "a sight of such common occurrence that it scarcely expects a passing notice," and she hoped "that the intelligent and moral only will find their way to Texas." [4]

Some of the pilgrims may have been intelligent and moral, but many, she found, lacked certain social graces: "On the other side of the Nueces is Oakville, a miserable settlement, consisting of about twenty wooden huts. We bought some butter there, and caught up with Ward's wagons. The women of Oakville were most anxious to buy snuff. It appears that the Texas females are in the habit of dipping snuff—which means putting it into their mouths instead of their noses. They rub it against their teeth with a blunted stick." [5]

The migration to the counties of Grayson, Hopkins, Kaufman, and Lamar came primarily from Missouri (18.8 percent), Tennessee (19.6 percent), and Arkansas (17.5 percent). Growth jumped by almost 20,000 immigrants in 1859–60 as the nation headed for division.

And again, in 1850, perhaps Miss Rankin saw what she wanted to see: "It is not an inferior order of citizens who come to Texas. Men of wealth, talent, and influence compose the more recent class of immigrants, who are well calculated to advance the interest of a new and growing state."

And it was, to some extent, true. Most of the settlers were honest folks, determined to escape the ravages of war and atrocities by the border ruffians on both sides and to avoid the conflicts that shattered families in the border states, particularly in Missouri and Kansas. But they were just the forerunners of the population explosion that would take place as the Civil War droned into its third year, when the quality of immigrants declined tremendously.

Religion in the days before the Republic was sparse, except of course, for the Catholic Church, which controlled South Texas and the predominantly Mexican population. After the victory at San Jacinto, the Protestant denominations began to organize, and a number of camp meetings and Bible schools were held before 1836.

Stephen F. Austin wrote as early as 1824 in the Austin papers: "There are two obstacles which hinder immigration to this province; One is the doubt which exists concerning slavery and the other religion." Austin feared that a Protestant influx into Texas would cause trouble with the Mexican government.

But they came anyway, and among the first were the Methodists, whom Austin frowned on. "In some instances they are too fanatic, too violent and too noisy . . . I assure you it will not do to have the Methodist excitement raised in the country."[6]

In 1837, the Methodists were followed by the Presbyterians. Many times joint services were held, and slaves attended the services or a special service was held for them later.

Soon the Methodists and Presbyterians were joined by the Baptists, and all three organized. The Methodists formed conferences, the Presbyterians presbyters, and the Baptists an association.

Other denominations joined in the rush to Texas. The Episcopalians were first represented by Rev. John Wurts Cloud from Georgia, who came to Texas in 1831, and included such luminaries as G. Leonidas Polk of North Carolina, who was appointed missionary bishop of the Southwest in 1838. He left that post to accept a general's commission in the Confederate army and was killed at Pine Mountain, Georgia, in 1864.

The Disciples were in Texas as early as 1824 and brought with them Collin McKinney, who was to become a leader in the growth of Texas. In 1841 the McKinney family located on Hickman's Prairie in what is now Bowie County.

A group of Mormons established a camp near Sherman at one time, but moved on to avoid persecution.

One of the outstanding Baptist preachers of the time was

Rev. James Huckins, who often preached to the slaves after holding services for the whites. Other outstanding pulpiteers included Martin Ruter, R.E.B. Baylor, and Sumner Bacon.

There were camp meetings, and preachers of the various denominations rode from city to city, carrying the Gospel in their saddlebags.

And there was plenty to preach against, from widespread gambling and dancing to the profusion of saloons and prostitution that flourished in almost every city.

As the preachers fanned the flames of revival, Texas began to change. In 1842, G. Gates, a visitor to northeast Texas, wrote: "I think that during my short visit there I saw as much practical living Christianity as I have a any time or in any place seen under like circumstances. The people in this part of Texas are not renegades. They are as honorable, intelligent, hospitable and well disposed, so far as I saw, and am able to judge, as any people that I have ever seen in a newly settled country; and I believe the gospel, properly presented, would be crowned with a great success in that Republic as anywhere else." [7]

Temperance societies were formed at Clarksville, Houston, and Corsicana. Even Sam Houston made a speech at one of the rallies, urging abstinence from drink. He did, however, suggest that his listeners do as he said and not as he had done.

Theaters were looked down on but not condemned entirely, but you could get ejected from the Baptist Church for drinking.

By 1855, there were 35,000 Protestant churches in Texas.[8]

In the years ahead, Texas would blossom with thousands of steeples, and the great revival at the close of the Civil War would result in the state becoming a part of the "Bible belt."

Meanwhile, when the Civil War came, even the major Protestant denominations could not stand the rendering within themselves and most of them, like the nation, split.

In his last speech in the United States Senate, John C. Calhoun stated in the debate over the Compromise of 1850 that "The cords which bind the states together are not only many but various in character. Some are spiritual or ecclesiastical, some political, others social." [9]

As the ecclesiastical cords began to snap, the others soon broke, both in Texas and in the nation.

In 1858, travelers and mail came across Texas from both directions when the John Butterfield Overland Mail Company sliced across the state, entering across Colbert's Ferry on the north and exiting near El Paso on its way eventually to San Francisco. On September 28 the first stage pulled up to the Jones Livery Stable on the Sherman Courthouse square.[10]

The mail service was halted in 1861 after Confederate guerrillas and Texas highwaymen found the stage and its stop stations easy pickings for loot and horses.

But Texas was also divided politically. Even the father of the Republic, Sam Houston, opposed secession and fought against it to no avail.

Divided north Texans grew anxious as they heard of the undeclared war on the border between "bleeding Kansas" and Missouri, and when the state passed the Texas Ordinance of Secession in 1861, eight northern counties, including Grayson, voted against withdrawing from the Union. The voting records show that on February 23, 1861, Collin County voted against secession, 405 to 948; the vote in Fannin County was 471 to 656; in Lamar County it was 553 to 663, and in Grayson County, the vote was 553 for, and 663 against."[11] In the southern tier of the state, the vote was entirely reversed as Brazoria County voted for secession, 527 to 2.[12]

On November 23, 1860, the citizens of Cooke and Grayson counties met at Whitesboro and passed a resolution: "Self preservation and absolute duty we owe to our homes, and firesides demand that we should look to our constitutional privileges from security and safety, instead of to the will of the majority of the people of the United States which has expressed under false teaching in the face of the Constitution."[13]

In January of 1861 a petition was circulated calling for northern Texas to form a separate state and remain in the Union. Those who favored secession believed that the Union could be dissolved legally and peacefully.

As in Missouri, neighbors turned on their neighbors as fear gripped the region, with even the churches and preachers becoming part of the division. There were constant rumors of slave insurrections, and the fires that broke out across the state only added to the fear.

On July 3, 1860, a fire ravaged the Dallas Town Square. Fires also blazed in Denton, Waxahachie, Jefferson, and Pilot Point. Citizens feared the worst, that slaves or northern abolitionists were torching the state. The record high temperatures, as high as 114 degrees in Hopkins County, plus the new-fangled phosphorous matches, known as prairie matches, were probably the culprits, but that did not prevent panic from controlling the citizens of north Texas.[14]

Rumors that free-soilers who had moved to Texas from northern border states had organized into what was known as the "Clan" or "Committee," a fraternal organization much like the Southern "Knights of the Golden Circle" and were planning an uprising that included a revolt of the slaves, caused Southern sympathizers to shudder and resulted in a vigilante committee being formed in Gainesville in Cooke County.

The Clan was infiltrated in spite of a system of signs which helped them identify one another. A member would draw his finger over his right ear, and the proper response was to draw a finger over the left ear. A handshake with the forefinger extended to the wrist and pressure applied confirmed the identification. If you asked someone where he obtained a certain item, such as a gun, horse, or saddle, and he answered "Arizona," you knew he was one of the Clan, unless of course he had really been to Arizona and obtained the item.

The vigilantes claimed they had uncovered a plot to take over Gainesville and Sherman by the Clan and began "arresting" suspected unionists in Gainesville. The court, which had no legal basis, convicted those accused over the objections of Church of Christ preacher and physician Thomas Barrett, who served on the jury. Barrett, along with other members of the kangaroo court, fled when the military declared martial law and issued warrants for their arrests. But not before forty-two men had been hanged from a large elm tree on the edge of Gainesville and two were shot trying to escape.[15] Forty others, arrested and doomed to hanging, were spared when legitimate Confederate forces interfered.

It was 1861, and the madness had only begun. In less than two years, Colbert's Ferry would become the small opening in a funnel through which flowed riff-raff, border ruffians, deserters from both armies, and escapees from persecution in Missouri and Kansas. And in the winter of 1863, a group known as guerrillas, raiders, or bushwhackers, led by William Clarke Quantrill, crossed the Red River into Texas.

Melinda Rankin would not have been happy with this group of migrants, even if they were to be just temporary Texans.

Far to the north, across Indian country, Union orders were issued that were to have a detrimental effect on Texas, and particularly Grayson County.

Order No. 10
Issued with the approval of General Schofield by General
Thomas Ewing, on August 18, 1863.
Such officers will arrest, and send to the district provost-marshal for punishment, all men (and all women not heads of families) who willfully aid and encourage guerrillas, with a written statement of the names and residences of such persons and of the proof against them. They will discriminate as carefully as possible between those who were compelled, by threats or fears, to aid the rebels and those who aid them from disloyal motives. The wives and children of known guerrillas, and also women who are heads of families and are willfully engaged in aiding guerrillas, will be notified by such officers to remove out of this district and out of the State of Missouri forthwith. They will be permitted to take, unmolested,their stock, provisions, and household goods. If they fail to remove promptly, they will be sent by such officers, under escort, to Kansas City for shipment south, with their clothes and such necessary household furniture and provision as may be worth removing.

Order No. 11
I. All persons living in Jackson, Cass, and Bates Counties, Missouri, and in that part of Vernon included in this district, except those living within one mile of the limits of Independence, Hickman's Mills, Pleasant Hill, and Harrisonville, and except those in that part of Kaw Township, Jackson County, north of Brush Creek and west of the Big Blue, are hereby ordered to remove from their present places of residence within fifteen days from the date hereof.

Those who, within that time, establish their loyalty to the satisfaction of the commanding officer of the military station nearest their present places of residence, will receive from him certificates stating the fact of their loyalty and the names of witnesses by whom it can be shown. All who receive certificates will be permitted to remove to any military station in this district, or to any part of the state of Kansas except the counties on the eastern border of the state. All others shall remove out of this district. Officers commanding companies and detachments serving in the counties named, will see that this paragraph is promptly obeyed.

II. All grain and hay in the field or under shelter, in the district from which the inhabitants are required to remove, within reach of military stations, will be taken to such stations, and turned over to the proper officers there; and report of the amount so turned over made to district headquarters specifying the name of all loyal owners and the amount of such produce taken from them. All grain and hay found in such district after the 9th of September next, not convenient to such stations, will be destroyed.

III. The provisions of General Order Number 10 from these headquarters will be at once vigorously executed by officers commanding in the parts of the district and at the station not subject to the operations of Paragraph One of this order, and especially the towns of Independence, Westport, and Kansas City.

IV. Paragraph 3, Gen. Order No. 10 is revoked as to all who have borne arms against the Government in the district since the 20th day of August, 1863.

By Order of Brigadier General Thomas Ewing:
H. Hannahs, Adjutant General

CHAPTER 2

The Trip South

Their Federal uniforms were filthy but protected them from the coolness of the morning as the northwest winds had begun to blow in southwestern Missouri and their recent activities had brought the heat of criticism and revenge.

The only sounds were the creaking of the saddles and an occasional cough from the men who rode in a disorderly and unmilitary fashion through the damp Missouri dawn.

Just glancing at the motley group, one might think a Federal unit was on its way to southwest Missouri to track down and kill bushwhackers, but a closer look would reveal that most of the uniforms did not fit well and that the horses they rode were of much higher quality than Federal soldiers were furnished. An observer might even notice that several of the saddle horns had scalps hanging from them.

Underneath the blue coats, they wore the colorful shirts of the guerrillas, with four huge pockets that held extra ammunition for the two or more 1851 Navy Colts that were stuck in their belts.

Another method of telling they were not legitimate soldiers was the fact that no regimental or, for that matter, national flag was being displayed. Although a small flag (7" x 13") was found on the public square of Olathe, Kansas, by Jonathan Milliken after a raid by Quantrill, the only flag the bushwhackers normally flew was the American flag, and that only to make the enemy think they were Federals.

There were, among the renegades, some regular Confederate soldiers and recruits, but they were dressed in a hodge-podge of uniforms, or parts thereof, that gave them a very un-military air.

It was early fall of 1863 as they left the farm of Captain Perdee in Johnson County and headed for the warmer winds of northeast Texas and the relative comfort of their camp at Mineral Creek or the Ben Christian Hotel in Sherman.

It had not been a good year for the bushwhackers, unless you could call the massacre of innocents at Lawrence, Kansas, a victory. Some of the illegitimate Confederate soldiers did consider the revenge blow a tremendous victory, while others remained sickened by the madness of it.

Some could only think of their sisters and wives who had been killed in the collapsed "jail" in Kansas City. Whether the collapse occurred by accident or intent did not matter, for the guerrillas were convinced the Federals killed their loved ones on purpose. And it did not matter if your own sister or wife was there, for the possibility that they could have been was enough to make the hatred boil up inside all the men.

In retrospect, even the most critical reviewer of the guerrillas has to admit they had good cause to be not only angry, but tormented to the point of insanity.

It was a long ride to Texas, and there was to be more madness before they crossed the Kansas border, made their way through Indian Territory, and crossed the flat, muddy Red River, which formed the northern border of the Lone Star State.

Perhaps as many as 500 guerrillas (some reported fewer, and it was probably closer to 350) left the Perdee farm on October 2, 1863, at daylight. Their enemy in the next conflict would estimate the number at between 600 to 1,000, but Federal officers always greatly overestimated the number of guerrillas they faced. The guerrillas' last major action had been the rape of Lawrence, Kansas, where innocent men and boys were shot down and most of the town torched and stripped of valuables.

But the group that left Perdee's farm that October morning was a mix made up mostly of Quantrill's men, some civilians,

Confederate veterans who had been mustered out, and Col. John D. Holt and his recruits. They organized the First Regiment, First Brigade, Army of the South, and headed for Texas. Calling it a legitimate Confederate unit, led by duly processed officers, would most certainly be a stretch of the imagination.

Back in Missouri, they had felt the reprisal by the Federals for their action at Lawrence as Gen. Thomas Ewing issued Order No. 11, which very effectively and with much human suffering removed all Confederate sympathizers from the western border counties. Ewing, who had to answer to criticism for his lack of action by Senator James H. Lane, had allowed the fiery Kansas abolitionist to help him write the order in a little cabin. As they left, Lane said to Ewing, "You are a dead dog if you fail to issue that order as agreed between us."[1] His meaning, of course, was that he would destroy any hopes Ewing might have for future political success.

As it turned out, Ewing was damned if he did and damned if he didn't.

Not only were the people who had sheltered the guerrillas in the past gone, but so were most of their supplies, as crops were burned along with the homes of those loyal to the South. There were probably less than 10,000 citizens affected by the order in the sparsely settled countryside, but the impact on the guerrillas' mode of operation was dramatic. The brush men depended on their families and friends for food, a place to hide, and even ammunition.

The Federals were determined to avenge Lawrence, and the burned crops and devastated areas of the border counties, plus the increase in patrols by Union troops, made it a good time to decide to go to Texas, weather or not.

Now they rode past the charred remains of farmhouses, the blackened chimneys standing erect, monuments to Federal persecution. It was a surreal landscape, with burnt-off fields and woods. There was very little animal life, as all livestock had been carried off and much of the wildlife had moved on to greener pastures. In the still dawn, the silence must have been intense, punctuated perhaps by the occasional curse of one of the men as he saw his home, or that of a relative or friend, burned to the ground.

Quantrill had been able to incite the men to the Lawrence raid after the jail had collapsed on the bushwhackers' women, who had been imprisoned by the same Thomas Ewing.

"The large three-story brick building in the Metropolitan block, McGee's Addition, owned by G. C. Bingham, Esq., and occupied for the last two weeks as a guardhouse, fell in yesterday afternoon, carrying with it the adjoining building south. There were in the building at the time nine women prisoners, two children, and one man. Four women were killed, the balance escaped without fatal injuries."

Kansas City Daily Journal of Commerce, August 14, 1863:

"There was not a single Bushwhacker who did not believe that the Federals had deliberately undermined the foundation of the old brick structure, causing it to fall on the girls."

In his memoirs, John McCorkle gives the bushwhackers' version of the tragedy:

> . . .The girls had been uneasy by hearing the people on the floor below moving out their stock of groceries and whisky which they took to a safe place. The plastering had been falling all day and the girls were in a panic. Nan Harris and Mollie Anderson had just gone out into the hall for a bucket of water, when they heard cries from the other girls that the roof was falling. The guard, evidently repenting at the last moment if indeed there had been a conspiracy to kill the girls, carried these two girls to safety. Twelve year old Janie (or Jennie) Anderson, who was the youngest, tried to escape through a window, but a twelve pound ball that had been chained to her ankle held her back and both her legs were broken. She was in prison with her sisters because there was no one to take care of her. The ball had been placed on her leg because she had given the guards so much trouble. The other girls went down with the ruins. There were groans and screams for a long time, and Josephine Anderson could be heard calling for someone to take the bricks off her head. Finally her cries ceased.

Of course, William Connelley, who favored the Union side, reported it differently in *Quantrill and the Border Wars*:

"In 1863, General Ewing, in command at Kansas City, had

been compelled to arrest and imprison a number of young women living in Jackson County, Missouri. These women were spies, impelled by love for fathers, brothers, or sweethearts in the guerrilla camps." Connelley continues:

> Among these women were the sisters of Bill Anderson . . . three sisters, Josephine, Mary, and Jenny. They had been arrested south of Westport, near the state-line by a detail sent out for that purpose. Their arrest was accomplished with difficulty, for they fought like wildcats and screamed at their highest pitch . . . They dug under the foundation wall of that part of the building occupied by them and in one more night they would have dug their way out and have been free. But a windstorm came up and the building collapsed, killing a number of the women and wounding others.

There is no doubt that the women were guilty of aiding their men as much as possible and that they were indeed difficult to arrest and constrain—but a twelve-pound ball chained to the leg of a twelve-year-old girl?

And yet another view, given by Mattie Lykins, who was there:

> As a place of imprisonment for such in this city, an old dilapidated brick building on the levee . . . was taken possession of by the military authorities and set apart as a prison for rebel women. After the building had been occupied as such for some time it became so infested with rats and vermin of all kinds as to render it unfit for human beings to live in. Even the health of the guards, who had access to the river for bathing, suffered so much from the stench and torture of the vermin as to lead them to appeal to headquarters for a change of location. According to their request, a building was selected which stood about the middle of the block on Grand avenue between 13th and 14th streets. The house selected belonged to General Bingham . . .

Mattie went so far as to investigate the safety of this new prison: "The building had been weakened by the removal of the brick pillars which supported the first floor and furthers that some of the sleepers[3] of the adjoining buildings on both sides had also been removed." She reported that who had done this and for what purpose was not known, but "One hot day, about two o'clock, this prison fell, burying beneath its walls a number of its inmates, four of whom were dreadfully mangled and crushed."

As the bodies were being removed, Mattie stood beside Dr. Joshua Thorne, a surgeon at the hospital, and heard him say: "Not a bluecoat will be found; every man who had been detailed to stand guard at this prison for the last few days and weeks knew the house to be unsafe and have kept themselves at a safe distance from the trembling walls.

"I knew the building to be unsafe," he continued, "and notified the military authorities of the fact, and suggested the removal of the women prisoners, but my suggestion was not heeded and before you is the result."

And again, John McCorkle summed up the bushwhackers' feelings:

> We could stand no more . . . A loved sister foully murdered and the widow of a dead brother seriously hurt by a set of men to whom the name assassins, murderers and cutthroats would be a compliment . . . My God, did we not have enough to make us desperate and thirst for revenge? We tried to fight like soldiers, but were declared outlaws, hunted under a black flag and murdered like beasts. The homes of our friends burned, our aged sires who dared sympathize with us had been either hung or shot in the presence of their families and all the furniture and provisions loaded in wagons and with or without livestock taken to the state of Kansas. The beautiful farming country was worse than a desert, and on every hillside stood lone blackened chimneys, sad sentinels and monuments to the memory of our once happy homes . . . And now our innocent and beautiful girls had been murdered in a most foul, brutal, savage, and damnable manner. We were determined to have revenge.

According to McCorkle, the Lawrence massacre was a direct result of the prison deaths, but the fact is that Quantrill already had the raid planned, at least in his mind, to get revenge for the way Lawrence had expelled him earlier, and he used the deaths of the women to fan the bushwhackers' passion for the bloody atrocities against innocent men and boys.

It is true that the raiders found storehouses filled with loot that the Jayhawkers had carried to Lawrence from their Missouri raids on private citizens.

Some have claimed that Lawrence was meant to avenge the Federal raid on Osceola, but the true reason for the raid would be found in the warped mind of Quantrill. Whatever the reason for the massacre at Lawrence, the result was instrumental in sending the guerrilla gang south.

As the travelers to Texas camped out south of the Osage on the second night, most of them must have had their loved ones and friends who had lost everything on their minds.

But one of Quantrill's lieutenants, who until the "accident" at the jail had been known as William "Bill" Anderson, was on the verge of insanity and would soon go down in history as "Bloody Bill."

We can only imagine the anguish that Anderson and the others suffered, forced to ride to Texas for survival, leaving dead and wounded women behind them.

The band of guerrillas rode past Carthage and crossed Shoal Creek, following an old trail that led through part of Seneca country and eventually to Baxter Springs, Kansas. From there the trail ran due south and would take them to Texas.

But there was an obstacle in their path, one they did not even know about until they captured a lumber wagon driven by two Federals who said they were attached to the military post at Baxter Springs. After killing the wagoners, the guerrillas sent David Poole out to scout, and plans were made to attack the Federal position, known as Fort Blair.

Actually, it could hardly be called a fort. Earthernworks and logs and four log cabins, along with a dining brush arbor, made up the fortification. And even part of the earthernworks had been taken down so the fort could be expanded on orders of Lt. James B. Pond.[4]

At noon the guerrillas attacked, just as the Federals were having their lunch in the arbor, and they made a mad dash for the fort, actually running amid the guerrillas, who had overrun their position. With the help of a small howitzer, the Federal soldiers, which included the Second Kansas Colored Infantry, repelled the attackers.

While the attack was in progress, Gen. James G. Blunt, commander of the District of the Frontier and primary implementor of the "black flag" orders that designated guerrillas as non-military combatants who should be killed when captured, arrived four hundred yards from the fort and prepared for his entrance.

Blunt's communiqué as to the disposition of captured guerrillas had been explicit:

> I have instructed the officers in command of troops in the border counties of Missouri that every rebel, or rebel sympathizer, who gives aid, directly or indirectly, shall be destroyed or expelled from the military District. These instructions will not exempt females from the rule. Experience has taught that the bite of a she adder is as poisonous and productive of mischief as the bite of any other venomous reptile. Therefore all persons known to be in arms against the Federal authorities of this District, will be summarily put to death when captured. The only Constitutional right that will be granted them, will be the right to make choice of the quality of rope with which they will be hung.

Blunt was about to reap the backlash of this order.

Quantrill and his command had wandered from the fort and at this moment emerged from the woods. Since they were dressed in Federal blue, Blunt assumed they were an escort from the fort. Of course, the fact that they were displaying an American flag may have helped with the deception, too. Sitting in his carriage with a bottle of brandy and dressed in civilian clothes, Blunt was pleased. He ordered his band to the front of the column for the grand entrance.

Blunt called for a horse and rode out toward the line of bluecoats. But it didn't take long for the military man to notice that the soldiers in front of him were not acting as trained soldiers should, and he knew he was in trouble.

Something about the way the officers rode up and down the line did not look military to him, and suddenly he realized that they could very well be bushwhackers. Blunt ordered his escort into a battle line, sending the band and all other noncombatants to the rear.

At two hundred yards, Blunt could for the first time hear the firing from the battle at the fort, and at about the same time the guerrillas opened fire on him. Quantrill ordered a charge and the slaughter began.

By the time Blunt realized his mistake and turned back toward his own lines, he saw that his men had panicked and were in full flight. He later claimed that he had tried to reorganize the line and make a stand but was only able to rally fifteen men. Other reports implied that the good general, who had been sipping from the jug in his carriage, made a run to save his own skin.

The bushwhackers' superior horses and their ability to shoot their revolvers from the saddle at a gallop allowed them to catch the running Federals and shoot them from their mounts. In fifteen minutes, eighty-two Federals went down, dead or wounded.[5] Surrenders were not accepted, for as soon as the beaten soldiers handed over their weapons, they were shot. Blunt, seeing that the day—and his men—were lost, made a run for it and, thanks to a superior steed, escaped the carnage.

The band, dressed in fancy uniforms and wearing swords and revolvers, which apparently were mostly for show, tried to surrender, but one of them shot a guerrilla named William Bledshoe, and then they waved handkerchiefs at other bushwhackers, who surrounded their wagon.

Their surrender was to no avail, for George Todd gave them a good chewing out for shooting one of his men, and then all fourteen of them were shot. Their bodies were thrown under and on top of the wagon, which was then set on fire. Their twelve-year-old drummer boy, who had been wounded, crawled out of the fire with burning clothes for thirty yards before he died, leaving behind him a trail of scorched clothing bits. When he finally expired, only the cloth on his back, between him and the ground, was left.

Many of Blunt's men had whiskey in their canteens, and

Quantrill's men proceeded to get roaring drunk, including Quantrill himself, which was very unusual.

At one point, a guerrilla walked up to a Federal soldier's body and jocosely prodded him, urging the supposedly dead man to get to his feet. To his surprise, the soldier, who had been feigning death, jumped up, thinking his ruse had been discovered, and was promptly shot to death.

Another trooper was shot, and as he lay face down, one of the guerrillas jumped on his back and danced. Although it is not clear who the dancing guerrilla was, David Poole was known for counting the dead by jumping on them.

There had been reports of the mutilation of bodies back in Jackson County, but in his report, Maj. Benjamin S. Henning of the Third Wisconsin Cavalry may have reported the beginning of the guerrillas' love for mutilation, which was to reach a horrendous climax at a little town in Missouri called Centralia.

> A number of bodies were brutally mutilated and indecently treated . . . Some unarmed citizens that were with us were killed, and their bodies stripped of clothing. Take it all in all, there perhaps has not been a more horrible affair (except the massacre at Lawrence, Kansas) happened during the war, and brands the perpetrators as cowards and brutes. I will here also state that a woman and a child were shot at the camp; both will recover. It was done premeditatedly, and not by random shots, and the brute who shot the child was killed by a shot from the revolver of Sergeant McKenzie, Company C, Third Wisconsin Cavalry.[6]

After sending Todd back to the fort to demand a surrender from Lieutenant Pond, which was refused, Quantrill decided they had done enough damage for the day and once again turned south toward Texas, carrying their wounded in an ambulance wagon they had taken. His decision did not sit well with Bill Anderson, who wanted to kill as many Yankees as he could. It was not the last time they would disagree.

General Blunt had returned to Fort Blair and with a small force shadowed the guerrillas for some time, but he hesitated about attacking them and instead returned to the fort to lick his

wounds and bury his dead. And perhaps to think about the inquiry that would be held later to examine his actions at Baxter
Springs.

Quantrill failed to mention the murder of the band and the
twelve-year-old drummer in his report on the action, and of
course, they only thought they had killed the hated Blunt. The
officer they had shot from his horse was Major Curtis, the son of
Gen. Samuel Curtis, for Blunt was in civilian clothes and they
found his uniform and sword in the wagon.

On Sunday, October 11, 1863, the *New York Times* reported:

> The Democrat's (Leavenworth) special gives the particulars
> of the attack on Gen. Blunt and his escort below Fort Scott. He
> was attacked by 300 rebels in Federal uniform, near the en-
> campment of Lieut. Pond. His escort broke, and out of 100
> men, seventy-eight were killed—all shot through the head, ev-
> idently after they were captured.
>
> Maj. Curtiss, [*sic*] son of Gen. Curtiss, was thrown from his
> horse, and was found with a bullet-hole through his head. He
> was undoubtedly murdered after being taken prisoner. Lieut.
> Pond's camp was attacked about the same time. Four men were
> killed and three wounded.
>
> Gen Blunt escaped, and, meeting reinforcements below
> Fort Scott, took command of them and started in pursuit of
> Quantrell.
>
> Lieut. Foot, of the Third Missouri, was killed.
>
> Capt. Todd, Quantrell's Adjutant, came to Pond's camp and
> asked for an exchange of prisoners. He said a number of rebels
> were wounded, among them Col. Shelby.
>
> Quantrell's force came from Cowskin Prairie, McDonald
> County, Missouri.
>
> A letter from Fort Scott, 8th, says a rebel force burned
> Carthage, Mo. that morning.
>
> Gen. Schofield telegraphed to Leavenworth that from 1,000
> to 8,000 rebels, under Quantrell, Coffey, Gordon, and Hunter
> were marching on Fort Scott, and that he had ordered Col.
> Wise to move all the force he could raise to Fort Scott.

Quantrill would have probably had a good laugh if he had seen
this report, for the raiders never numbered in the thousands, except in the minds of the Yankee officers and press. The story, of

course, does not tell that Blunt deserted his command and ran
for his life.

But for Gen. Henry McCulloch down in Bonham, who was
nervous about a Federal invasion of Texas, the report was good
news, and he issued General Order No. 187:

> With much pleasure the major-general commanding makes
> known to the troops of this district the following cheering in-
> telligence from Northern Texas, congratulating them on the
> brightening of our prospects in that quarter: Very good news
> from our front. Brigadier-General Blunt, of the United States
> army, killed by Colonel (W. C.) Quantrill 30 miles from Fort
> Scott. The Federals fallen back. North Fork Town burned.
> Blunt had gone to Kansas, it is supposed, to organize and start
> his jayhawkers and Indians to the Texas frontier. On his return
> with his body-guard of 130 men, Quantrill attacked him,
> killing him, his adjutant-general, and many, if not all, of his
> men, capturing everything he had, including his sword, car-
> riage, &c. General Cooper advanced upon the enemy at North
> Fork Town, hoping to surprise them, but his advance was dis-
> covered, and the enemy fell back rapidly, burning the town
> when they left it. Our prospects are brightening in the north,
> thank God, and for the present, at least, Northern Texas is
> safe.[7]

General Blunt's account of the battle differs a great deal
from Quantrill's version, as would be expected. The account of
his arrival on the scene is pretty much the same, but from that
point, it sounds like an entirely different engagement. Blunt
tells of riding out in advance and discovering that it was rebel
and not Federal troops, and then stated:

> Being no longer in doubt that they were rebels, I turned to-
> ward my escort to give the command to fire, when I discovered
> the line broken, and all of them in full gallop over the prairie,
> completely panic-stricken . . .
> In vain I endeavored, with the assistance of Major Curtis,
> my assistant adjutant-general, to halt and rally the escort, and
> succeeded only in rallying 15 men, after following them one

and one-half miles. When turning upon them with this small force, they retreated back over the ground which they came, and formed in line upon the main road. After sending Lieutenant Tappan, of my staff, with 6 men to Fort Scott for troops, with the remaining nine men I kept close to them, watching their movements closely, which, doubtless, impressed them with the belief that I had a larger force coming up, as they burned all the wagons, and moved hurriedly off south, on the Fort Gibson road.

On looking over the ground for the wounded, I soon discovered that every man who had fallen, except 3, who escaped by feigning death, had been murdered, shot through the head. The brigade band, teamsters, and all headquarter's clerks who were first captured were murdered in the same way. On reaching Lieutenant Pond's camp, I found the command all safe.

Blunt added in his report: "Had the escort stood their ground and fought instead of running, I have no doubt that I could have driven them in a few minutes, and with the addition of Lieutenant Pond's cavalry, pursued and captured many of them."[8]

McCulloch could thank God for Quantrill after the victory, but in a few short weeks, he would regret welcoming the Missouri terrorists into his field of command. It is also interesting to note that the general referred to the guerrilla leader as "Colonel W. C. Quantrill," a title President Jefferson Davis had refused to bestow on him because Quantrill would not guarantee that prisoners would not be executed. The rank of colonel was awarded him by his men, or himself.

The guerrillas elected their own officers and Quantrill had no formal commission from the Confederacy, although officers were appointed by some commanders, such as the bestowal of the rank of major on Sam Hildebrand by Jeff Thompson, a commission that Sam could not even read and that was meaningless, since Thompson was not yet a member of the regular Confederate army.

After crossing the Arkansas River near Fort Gibson, the guerrillas captured twelve Indian soldiers and shot them after they had surrendered. Quantrill's report on the incident read: "We brought none of them through."

After Lawrence and Baxter Springs, Federal reports and

citizens began to refer to the bushwhackers as "demons," "devils," and "fiends."

They rested in the camp of Gen. Douglas H. Cooper, and Quantrill wrote his report on the action at Baxter Springs. In a few days, Quantrill finally took his irregular troops across the Red River at Colbert's Ferry and, after camping on the outskirts of Sherman for a few days more, moved into camp at Mineral Creek, about fifteen miles northwest of Sherman, leaving behind a trail of blood from Kansas to Texas, where the guerrillas decided to give up fighting for a while.

Except among themselves.

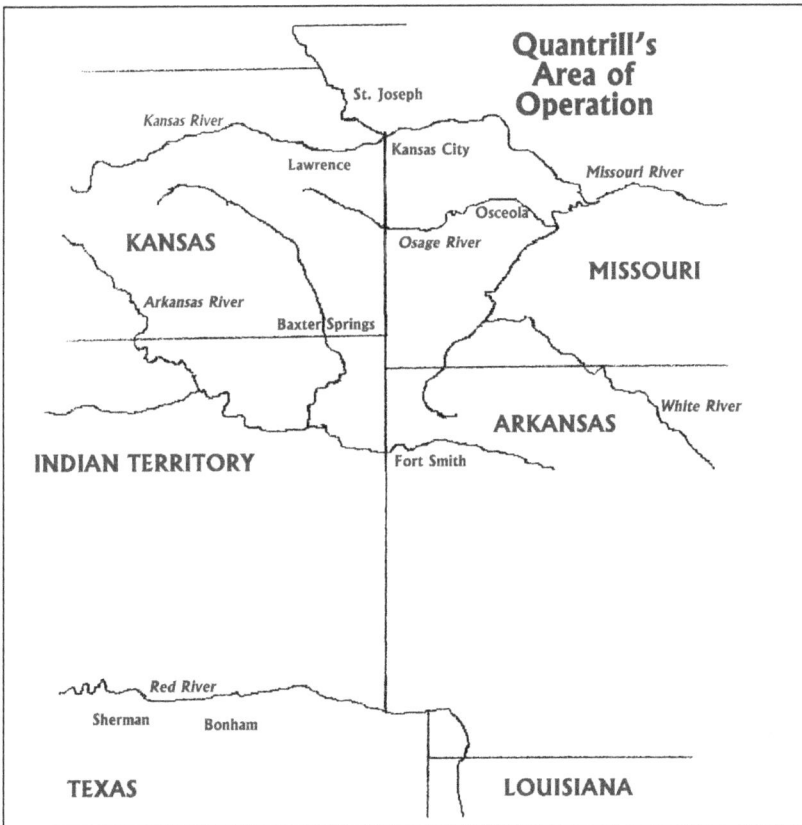

Map of Quantrill's area of operation in Kansas, Missouri, Indian Territory (now Oklahoma), Arkansas, Texas, and Louisiana. Public indignation over the slaughter of innocents at Lawrence, Kansas, coupled with Order No. 11, which removed his supporters from the border counties of southwest Missouri, influenced the guerilla to make the trek to Texas. —Map by Evault Boswell

CHAPTER 3

The Bushwhackers

There were almost as many reasons for becoming a bush-whacker as there were bushwhackers. Most of the men who took to the brush to fight an undefined war in an unorthodox manner had a grudge, either against the Federals, the Jayhawkers, or their own people. The number-one reason for bushwhacking was probably revenge.

There were others, wild young men, who could not tolerate the discipline of the regular army or who reveled in the excitement of riding hard and killing without purpose or reason. And after all, anything beat following a plow behind a Missouri mule.

There were those, of course, who had embraced the Southern cause and could be considered patriots of the South, but they were a minority.

Kansas Jayhawkers, bent on breaking the backs of the secessionists in western Missouri, seemed to have a hard time telling their friends from their enemies and in the process created a great number of bushwhackers.

In a letter to Edward Bates, attorney general of the United States, Richard C. Vaughan wrote on August 28, 1863:

> It is a fact well known to me that hundreds of the people of Jackson and Cass Counties are true and loyal men; they have already been robbed of their property, insulted, and in many

instances murdered by these troops from Kansas. The policy pursued has caused hundreds of good men to leave their homes and fly to the bushes for protection, while others have actually joined the guerrillas as a measure of safety, believing that they would be less liable to danger there than at their homes. These are generally men of little intelligence, who do not take consequences into consideration, and are not prompted by a very high order of patriotism; they act from motives of present interest, and for the temporary safety of their persons have been induced to commit a great crime against their country.[1]

Many unionists in Missouri used the excuse of war to root out their personal enemies, while others saw the opportunity to turn a fast Yankee dollar at the expense of those who professed to be Southern sympathizers.

The robbery and murder that took place early in the war in the name of preserving the Union were rampant, and "confiscation" became a household word as farms of Southerners were stripped of crops and livestock to support the vast blue army that flooded the state.

But before the real war began, the Kansas Jayhawkers waged their own crusade against Missourians, particularly slaveholders. However, loyal unionists were not immune to the thievery by the outlaw forces of Kansas. When the guerrillas raided Lawrence, they found warehouses filled with property stolen from the other side of the border.

Resistance to the stealing could only bring more reprisals, including death, down on the heads of citizens. Association with the guerrillas already in the hills could only mean more persecution for the families and friends, and contributed to the number of bushwhackers the Federals had to deal with. It was indeed a vicious circle.

There were also those who became guerrillas simply because they did not understand, or didn't want to participate in, the war as it was being fought by the organized armies of the South.

Most of the farm boys who fought in the brush wanted to ride fast horses, shoot pistols, and charm pretty girls and had no desire to spend hours on the drill field learning to be soldiers.

Sam Hildebrand, from southeast Missouri, was one who felt that the guerrillas' style of warfare was much more effective:

> A necessity as implacable as the dress of Fate: was forced upon me by the Union party to espouse the opposite side; and all the horrors of a merciless war were waged unceasingly against me for many months before I attempted to raise my hand in self defense. But fight I must, and fight I did! War was the object, and war it was. I never engage in but one business at a time—my business during the war was killing enemies. It is a very difficult matter to carry on a war for four years without some one getting hurt. If I did kill over a hundred men during the war, it was only because I was in earnest and supposed that everybody else was. My name is cast out as evil because I adopted the military tactics not in use among large armies. They were encumbered with artillery and fought where they had ample room to use it. I had no artillery and generally fought in the woods; my plan was the most successful, for in the regular army the rebels did not kill more than one man each during the war.[2]

Sam spent most of the war killing his personal enemies, members of the vigilantes who had killed three of his brothers, one of them only twelve years old, and forced his mother out of her home. At the close of the conflict, Sam had carved ninety-two notches on the stock of his gun, "Killdevil."

Almost every bushwhacker had a tale of horror to tell about the persecution of their family for favoring the Southern cause and, if they did not, made one up, as William Quantrill did.

A great many of the bushwhackers were little more than children. Allen Parmer and Jesse James were young teenagers when they started riding with Quantrill just before the Lawrence massacre.

There were a few who just enjoyed killing people. George Todd and Archie Clements were perhaps mentally ill. Clements was known for mutilation, from scalping his victims to taking strips of their skin. At the Centralia massacre, heads of the dead were cut off and placed on other bodies.

Hildebrand's habit of hanging his victims, using the strips of bark from a hickory tree, meant they died from strangulation, and was just one more example of the cruelty that was manifested in the guerrilla warfare.

The Official Records, Series 1, Volume XXII, page 80, has a vivid description of what guerrilla warfare could be like, in a letter addressed to Gen. Samuel Curtiss on January 27, 1863:

"You know that the whole western country is filled with guerrillas, who are carrying on a most bloody and cruel warfare. You know of those men of the Fifth Regiment, who were most cruelly assassinated by the guerrillas in Jackson County, and their bodies most horribly mutilated, even to stamping with boot-heels the flesh from their faces, cutting off their ears, pouring powder into their ears and exploding it."

The absolution of slavery, or for that matter, politics in general, was a minor issue as far as bushwhacking was concerned. The politicians such as Sterling Price were fighting in the regular Confederate army. Jeff Thompson, the mayor of St. Joseph, Missouri, chose to fight the guerrilla war in the beginning but later joined the regular Confederate troops.

The men shooting from ambush, for the most part, had no slaves and were never proactive in politics, even on a local level. Somehow the "cause" had an entirely different meaning to them. It was a personal war that would not end until all their real and imagined enemies were killed, or they were. For the most part, it was to be them.

Following is a list of some of the main characters and a thumbnail sketch of their lives and their involvement with Quantrill, particularly in the winter of 1863, when the Southern city of Sherman, Texas, was to reap the whirlwind of their madness.

These are not intended to be complete biographies of the participants, but only to give the reader an understanding of who these men where and at least some insight into their personalities.

Also listed are some of the military, both North and South, who played a role in the events that took place in Texas in 1863–64.

The Bushwhackers

WILLIAM T. ANDERSON

Better known as Bloody Bill

His parents, William and Martha, had six children, including Bill's two brothers, Ellis and James, and three sisters, Mary Ellen, Josephine, and Janie. Another brother, Charles, was born while the family lived in Kansas and probably died as a child.

The senior Anderson left his home in Kentucky, moved his family to Missouri, and, after sojourns in Missouri and Iowa, went to California in search of gold but found none and returned to his home near Huntsville, Missouri.

The family moved to a claim of the elder Anderson's, thirteen miles from Council Bluffs, Kansas. In the census of 1860, the farm contained one horse, two cows, and a team of oxen, and consisted of 320 acres. It was valued at $1,000.

But trouble for the Andersons came in short order. Brother Ellis killed an Indian and fled to Iowa to avoid prosecution, and Martha, at the age of thirty-six, was struck by lightning and killed.

Many of the men who became bushwhackers did so because they believed in the cause of the South, they had a family cause to avenge, or they were greedy for loot and enjoyed killing.

Bill Anderson was one of the latter. He made up a story about his father and uncle being hanged as Southern sympathizers, in order to give credibility to his devotion to the cause, when in fact he was little more than a horse thief and a cold-blooded killer from the beginning. But his story about his father was believed by his fellow bushwhackers and even some later historians.[3] He could not foresee at the beginning of his journey as a guerrilla that eventually the Federals would give him an honest reason for revenge.

In 1861, while trying to persuade a neighbor to join his band, Anderson said: "I don't care any more than you for the South, Strieby, but there is a lot of money in this (bushwhacking) business."

As for his father's death, it came at the hands of a bridegroom who had his wedding day interrupted by an attack on his home by the drunken senior Anderson.

Arthur Baker had founded Agnes City, Kansas, and named it after his mother in 1856, owning every building in town including his two-story stone home. He had been postmaster, justice of the peace, and a judge. In 1861 he established the *Council Grove Press* and a hotel, but neither proved profitable and he sold them at a loss the same year.

He had also lost a crop on his farm and most of his cattle, and since Jayhawking had come to be almost considered an almost honest and certainly a profitable enterprise, he formed a band for that purpose, including Bill Anderson and his eighteen-year-old brother, James.

Once again, a business endeavor of Baker's failed and a Union patrol, mistaking them for Missouri bushwhackers, attacked them, capturing Baker, who spent the rest of 1861 in prison at Fort Scott, Kansas.

He was released on March 24, 1862, and returned home to lick his wounds. Having lost his wife, he decided to court Anderson's fifteen-year-old sister, Mary Ellen.

The courtship grew hot and heavy, and soon the Andersons became convinced that Baker would marry their little sister, but Baker jilted her for a seventeen-year-old schoolteacher named Annis Segur, and the males in the Anderson family expressed their rage.

Baker soon rubbed salt into their open wound by forming a posse and arresting a cousin for stealing horses. Dumping Mary Ellen had been bad enough, but accusing one of the family of being a horse thief (which the Andersons apparently considered an honest occupation) brought out the worst in William Anderson Sr.

On the day of Baker's wedding to the lovely Annis, William Senior loaded his double-barreled shotgun, stopped at Baker's store to have another shot of whiskey, and headed for the Baker house. He did not know that Eli Sewell, seeing the drunken condition of Anderson, had removed the caps from his gun, preventing it from being fired.

It did not matter, as it turned out, for when William arrived at the home, Baker was upstairs getting ready for his wedding and heard the ruckus downstairs.

He met William as he started up the stairs with his own shotgun and promptly blew a hole in his chest and went on with his wedding plans.

Expecting the Anderson brothers to come for him, Baker had a posse formed, led by Charles Strieby, and Bill was arrested for stealing horses but was released on bond and loaded what was left of the Anderson family in a wagon and moved to Missouri.

Of course, Baker expected retaliation from the Anderson boys and should have been on guard when a stranger banged on his door late at night, claiming to be the leader of a wagon train and wanting to buy some whiskey.

The sleepy Baker and his brother-in-law, sixteen-year-old George Segur, opened the store and, finding no whiskey on the shelves, went through a trap door to the cellar to restock.

Baker filled a bottle and turned to find himself facing Bill and Jim Anderson. Baker said he wasn't expecting him, which was obvious, and Bill shot him in the thigh. Some reports say Bill or Jim also wounded the young Segur, but it really didn't matter, for leaving the basement, they closed the trap door, piled stock on top of it, and set the building on fire.

They stayed and watched for a while but became bored and torched Baker's house and barn and rode off into the darkness.

Baker was found the next morning in the ashes, but death had not come from the wound in his leg or the flames, for he had put his pistol to his head and shot himself to avoid the suffering in the fire. Segur managed to escape the dungeon but was badly burned and died the next day.

And now the Andersons became full-time bushwhackers, formed their own gang of cutthroats, and began spreading terror on both sides of the border until William Quantrill got word that the Anderson boys were showing no difference between the Southerners and the unionists. He sent a squad to take away their horses and gave them a warning to leave Southern folk alone or they would be killed, a threat Bill Anderson never forgot, even after he began to ride with Quantrill. It was a silent grudge, inflamed by other differences, that was to bubble to the top while the raiders were in Texas.

But there were three more incidents that were to shape the mind of the man who was to become known later as "Bloody Bill."

The first started with the arrest, ordered by Gen. Thomas Ewing, of those assisting the bushwhackers, including the sisters of Anderson, who were then locked up in the jail in Kansas City. The second was the sacking of Lawrence, Kansas, a vengeful plan by Quantrill, who used the jail deaths, whether they were intentional or accidental, to work his guerrillas into a frenzy that climaxed in the greatest atrocities of the war.

Many of Anderson's followers had doubts about his sanity before the death of Josephine, but now many were certain that he was indeed a madman who cared not if he lived or died and recklessly risked his life and the lives of his band to kill Federals.

In Texas, over the objection of Quantrill, Anderson married Bush Smith, a local hooker, according to most historians. However, Bush was listed as a member of the local Methodist Church, which would hardly have been possible for a prostitute. The wedding ceremony was performed by M. Y. Brockett. Connelley states that the marriage took place soon after their arrival in Texas, but the marriage license for Lt. Bill Anderson and Bush Smith was issued in March of 1864, more than six months after Bill arrived.

JOHN MCCORKLE

One of Quantrill's bushwhackers who lived to tell about it

Born in Andrew County, Missouri, McCorkle began the war serving in the Missouri State Guard and fought with Sterling Price at Lexington.

Captured and released by the Federals after taking the oath not to fight anymore, McCorkle reneged on his pledge when pro-Union neighbors began to harass him and his family and the Union army insisted he prove his allegiance by joining the state militia.

Singing a simple little song got John in trouble with the

Federals, who took offense to the lyrics they heard him singing as he passed them:

"We'll hang John Brown on a sour apple tree
And feed Jeff Davis on peaches and cream."

When they threatened to imprison a cousin, Mollie Wigginton, McCorkle, along with his long-range rifle, became a member of Quantrill's raiders and was immediately promoted to sniper and scout.

From the beginning, McCorkle's allegiance to Quantrill was unquestioned. He always refers to the leader as "Colonel" Quantrill in his book *Three Years with Quantrill*. The relationship was strained on several occasions, when according to McCorkle he failed to carry out Quantrill's orders and was threatened with being shot.

As late as the battle at Baxter Springs, there was conflict when McCorkle mistakenly thought Quantrill said he was going to shoot him, when in fact the guerrilla leader was offering him a drink from General Blunt's captured bottle of brandy—or at least that was Quantrill's claim when McCorkle drew his revolver on him.

JESSE JAMES

Was he a modern-day Robin Hood, a cold-blooded killer, or both?

So much has been written about Jesse James that it has become difficult to tell the difference between history and imagination. Because of the nickel and dime pulps and Hollywood's portrayals over the years, to most of the public, Jesse has become a legend, the reincarnation of Robin of Sherwood Forest, dashing about the countryside on a fire-breathing stallion, taking from wealthy bankers and railroad presidents and giving the money to poor postwar Missourians.

Not nearly as much has been written about the factors that caused a sixteen-year-old farm boy to become a notorious guerrilla, killer, and train and bank robber, the hero of thousands and the terror of many others.

It is said that imitation is the epitome of respect, and if that is true, Jesse became one of the most respected men of all time, for over the years, since his death on April 3, 1882, when Bob Ford shot him and he was buried in Kearney, Missouri, a number of men have come forward, one as late as 1951, claiming to be Jesse James.

Perhaps the best known of these was J. Frank Dalton, who died in 1851 in Texas. In the 1953 book *The Complete and Authentic Life of Jesse James,* Carl Breihan used the entire first chapter, fourteen pages, to prove that Dalton was not Jesse, something that even a casual historian didn't need proven. J. Frank Dalton may have ridden with Quantrill, but he was not Jesse James.

But even in recent years, Waggoner Carr, former attorney general of the state of Texas and a relative of Dalton's, brought back the haunting refrain that Dalton was indeed the real Jesse James, living in hiding in Texas for many years before going public to sell his identity to any cave owner in the country that would hire him to claim he hid out in that particular cave. He was even invited to Northfield, Minnesota, to help celebrate the famed robbery that went awry in that city.

In the book *Jesse James Lived and Died in Texas,* Betty Dorsett Duke presented some very convincing family history and photos to prove that her great-grandfather, James L. Courtney, was the real Jesse and lived in Blevins, Texas. I have met Mrs. Duke and am convinced of one thing: she believes James L. Courtney was Jesse James. But her assumptions are based mostly on family tradition, with very little support from a historical paper trail.

The real Jesse James, like so many Missourians, could trace his roots back to Kentucky, where his father, Robert James, a Baptist preacher, married Zerelda Cole, who was a Catholic nun, on December 20, 1841. Robert was twenty-three years old and Zerelda was seventeen, well past marrying age for a Kentucky lass.

The union produced three children. Frank was born on January 10, 1844, after the family had moved to Clay County in Missouri. Jesse Woodson James was born on September 5, 1847, and sister Susan first saw light on November 25, 1849.

Their father, in search of gold and souls, journeyed in 1851 to fabled California, where he developed a fever and died shortly after his arrival. But in 1852, Zerelda found a new father for her little family, a farmer named Benjamin Simms. After his untimely death, Zerelda remained twice-widowed until 1857, when she married Dr. Reuben Samuels.

Like so many other farm boys, the James brothers neither understood nor wanted any part of the battle between the states, although their family owned slaves. They were happy hunting the wilds of western Missouri and farming the fertile soil.

But between the Jayhawkers, the Redlegs, and the Quantrill bushwhackers, there was little room for neutrality, especially in the home of Dr. Samuel, who was of strong Southern sympathies.

When a group of militia came to the Samuels' farm searching for Frank, who had joined the dreaded Quantrill, they hanged Dr. Samuels by his neck in an effort to get him to tell the whereabouts of the guerrilla. In spite of severe rope burns on his neck, Samuels survived. Jesse was jabbed with bayonets and beaten with a rope, but he either did not know or would not tell where Quantrill and Frank were. But soon after that he was placed in jail in Liberty, Missouri, and upon his release, continued to farm for a year before riding to join his brother Frank at the ripe old age of sixteen.

Jesse's activities in the Lawrence raid have been exaggerated, if not invented altogether. In *The Life, Times, and Treacherous Death of Jesse James,* by Frank Triplett, written in 1882, it is stated that "in this attack, Jesse James is said to have killed thirty men, thus running his score up to this time about one hundred." That, of course, is a ridiculous exaggeration of Jesse's exploits at the age of sixteen.

Carl Breihan, in *Quantrill and His Civil War Guerrillas,* says that Jesse was a new recruit and Quantrill had refused to let him go on the raid.

Albert Castel, in *William Clarke Quantrill: His Life and Times,* does not mention Jesse but lists Frank and Cole Younger as new recruits.

John Burch, a guerrilla who rode with the James boys, relates a story in which Jesse's baby face was used to kill a group of Union soldiers, even if he did have to dress up like a woman. Jesse, wearing a dress and bonnet, supposedly enticed the soldiers to a remote cabin where the bushwhackers shot them like fish in a barrel.

The names of Jesse and Frank James are hardly mentioned in reports of the bushwhackers' trip to northeast Texas in 1863, but there is evidence that they were there, since their younger sister taught school in Sherman after the war, married one of the bushwhackers, and settled in Texas until her death in 1889.

ALEXANDER FRANKLIN JAMES

Jesse's big brother, and an enigma in his own right

Frank James was only thirteen when the border wars broke out in 1856, and he grew up learning to hate Jayhawkers and Redlegs. His parents, Robert and Zerelda, had moved to Missouri from Kentucky in 1842 and had three children, Frank, Jesse, and Susan.

Frank left their farm in Clay County and joined the state guard to fight with Sterling Price at the Battle of Wilson's Creek as a member of the militia, along with Cole Younger, but soon after became ill with measles. Captured at Springfield, he took an oath not to fight against the United States again.

The tall, thin farm boy with gray eyes joined Quantrill in the brush, and it was his involvement with the guerrilla leader that brought the wrath of the military down on the rest of the James family.

At the Battle of Prairie Grove, he was credited with helping to save Jo Shelby from capture, and he was one of the principal characters at Lawrence.

SAM HILDEBRAND

Did he really ride with Quantrill?

In Carl Breihan's book *Quantrill and His Civil War Guerrillas*, not only was Sam Hildebrand listed as one of Quantrill's men, but Sam's picture (according to Breihan) was superimposed be-

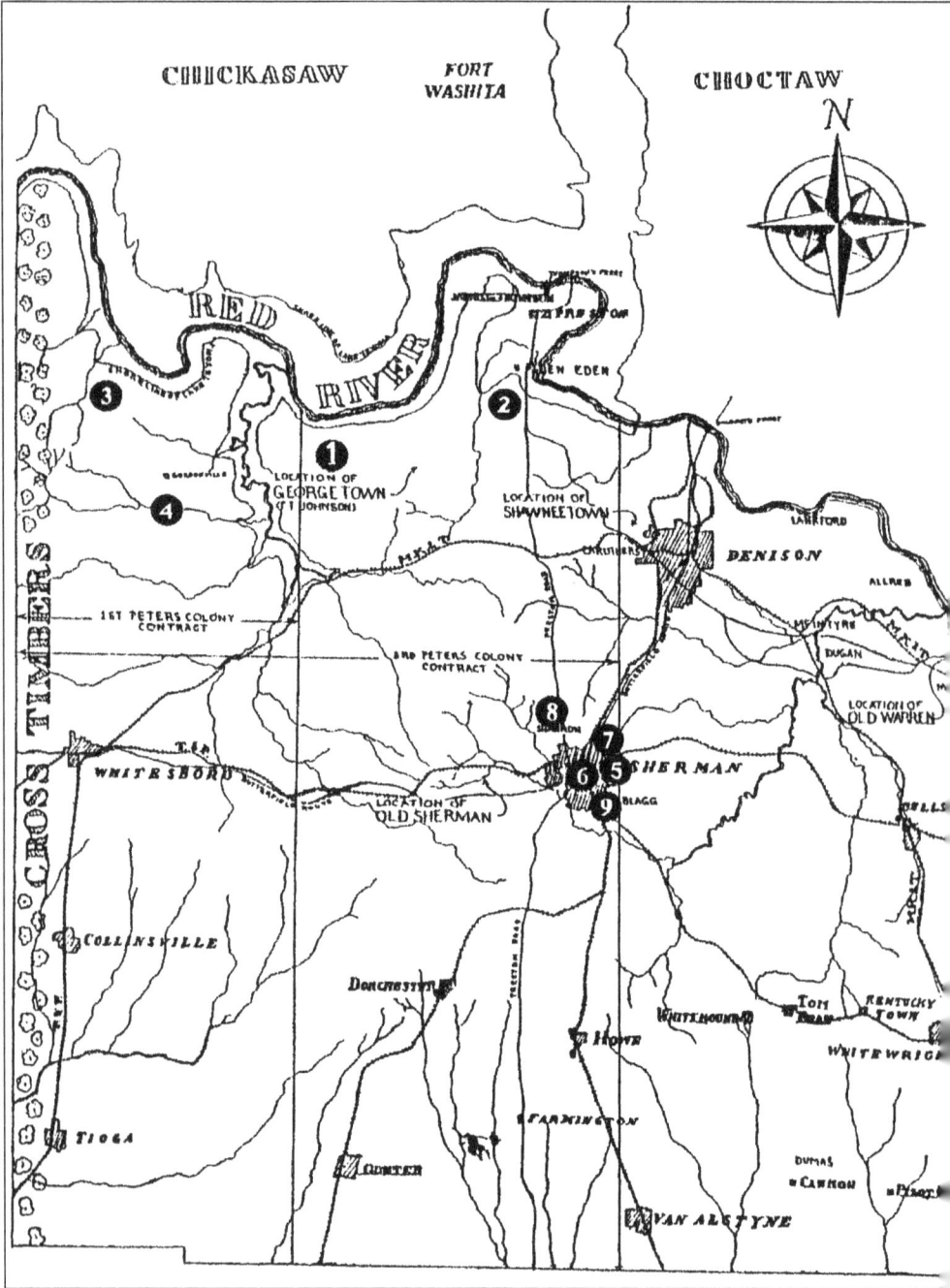

—Courtesy the Red River Historical Museum

42

MAP GUIDE

1. *Main Quantrill campsite and later outlaw hideout just southeast of where Big Mineral Creek flowed into the Red River, on Brogdon Springs just east of the Bounds Ferry Road and one mile due south of the ferry. Map coordinates are: 96.71936 longitude, 33.81065 latitude. The 11th Texas Confederate Cavalry was organized here, and the 5th Texas Partisan Rangers were often deployed here.*
2. *Approximate location of Glen Eden northwest of Grandpappy Point. This was the home of Sophie Porter, noted as the Texas "Confederate Lady Paul Revere."*
3. *Skirmish with Comanche war party in October 1863.*
4. *Silas Gordon, namesake of Gordonville, abandoned his life as a guerrilla with Quantrill in 1864 and returned to Texas to settle here, raising mules and jackasses on a large scale.*
5. *The home of newlyweds Bill Anderson and Sherman girl Bush Smith at 1312 E. Cherry in Sherman.*
6. *Scene of violent spree by groups of Quantrill's guerrillas in downtown Sherman on Christmas Eve, 1863, at Ben Christian's Hotel near the Butterfield Stage stop. Near here was the Confederate commissary where Quantrill faced down a crowd of angry, armed, and hungry women without a shot being fired.*
7. *Rendezvous point near current College and Broughton streets, used primarily by Bill Anderson, Fletch Taylor, and others plotting against Quantrill in late 1863.*
8. *Murder and apparent robbery in 1863 of Major Butt, Sophie Porter's husband, on his way home from Sherman after selling a cotton crop. Quantrill lieutenant Fletch Taylor is accused and confesses but says it was on Quantrill's orders. Taylor, however, was reported to be elsewhere by other guerrillas at the time of the Butt killing.*
9. *Location of Allen Parmer/Susan James homestead in 1876. E/S Broughton between King and Center streets. Parmer was listed as a farmer in the 1876–77 Mooney & Morrison's City Directory, published 1876.*

hind that of Quantrill on the cover, despite the fact Sam was not mentioned in the book.

However, in his 1984 book *Sam Hildebrand, Guerrilla,* Breihan included an introduction written by Edward McArtor, who stated that his father, James T. McArtor, rode with Sam a number of times, and gave accounts of guerrilla encounters in Jackson County, Missouri, and his return with Sam from Kansas to Quantrill's camp.

The rest of Breihan's book did not include any account of Sam having fought with Quantrill but was primarily a paraphrasing of Sam's own memoirs, which made no mention of Sam's presence in Jackson County.

McArtor gave a relatively accurate account of the Battle of Pilot Knob, Missouri, in September of 1864, stating that the story was told to him by his father, who rode with Sam. The fact is that Sam neither saw nor participated in the battle but was running a lead mining operation near his home territory of Big River Mills, more than thirty miles away.

Quantrill, at that time, had reunited with Anderson and Todd to be the advance guard for Price's army in his ill-fated invasion of Missouri, and the guerrillas were active in central Missouri, although, as always, they seemed to be more interested in loot than in the Confederate cause.

Hildebrand, one of the lesser known of the bushwhackers, probably never rode with Quantrill personally, since most of his activities took place in southeast Missouri. In his memoirs, *Confessions of Sam Hildebrand,* which he dictated to Dr. Abram Keith and a Mr. Evans in 1870, Sam never mentioned riding with Quantrill, although he did report one raid to west Missouri, in the area of Springfield, but that was with some of his own men, along with Quantrill's. It ended in disaster when a spy led the Federals to their camp and Sam escaped afoot and headed for his headquarters in Greene County, Arkansas. Sam vowed never again to go into areas of the state he was not familiar with.

Connelley's book *Quantrill and the Border Wars* barely mentioned Hildebrand, only saying that "Quantrill, Todd, Gordon, Hildebrand, Porter, and many others perpetrated deeds in Missouri against Missourians as brutal as any others did and as inhuman as could be conceived by the savage Indians of the plains in their wildest and bloodiest days. And their justification for such a course was that their brother Missourians stood for the Union."[4] Connelley almost always seemed to overlook the injustices done to Southern sympathizers by the Federal authorities.

Sam Hildebrand rarely fought with large forces but traveled into St. Francois County, Missouri, for the purpose of avenging wrongs committed against himself and his family by the home guard vigilantes and the Federal troops.

Brownlee's *Gray Ghosts of the Confederacy* and Castel's *William Clarke Quantrill* fail to mention Hildebrand.

He was certainly not in Texas in 1863, for he stayed at winter headquarters at Crowley's Ridge in Greene County, Arkansas, and continued to make raids into southeast Missouri. On November 25, 1863, Hildebrand captured Farmington, Missouri, as described in a letter by a Captain Rice: "Hildebrandt [*sic*] with 20 men, plundered Farmington this afternoon, and left with their pillage on the Jackson Road about 4 o'clock. I think you can certainly catch him. Strike swiftly. Keep (George W.) Hummell. Get horses for his men, if possible, and don't stop until you kill these rascals. Go at once. Kill them as you find them."[5]

Hildebrand does, however, have a Texas connection. After the war, with a price on his head and chased by Pinkerton detectives across Arkansas and Missouri, he finally took his family to Sherman, Texas. His wife, Margaret, died during the trip and was buried along the trail.

Sam probably killed more men than Quantrill, for when the fight was over, his rifle, "Killdevil," had ninety-two notches carved on the stock, more than Bill Anderson's famed knots in a silken rope.

ALLEN PARMER

Jesse James' brother-in-law

Very little is known about the early life of Allen Parmer. He became acquainted with the James boys when he was fifteen years old and was smitten by their little sister, Susan, whom he would later marry.

Jesse, who was sixteen when the Lawrence raid took place, was too young to take part in the campaign, which would cast doubt on whether or not Parmer was there.

But the *Dallas Morning News* reported on November 27, 1927, that Parmer, one of only seven remaining Quantrill's Raiders, had passed away on October 25 in Wichita Falls, Texas, and gave a vivid account of his actions at Lawrence:

> Allen Palmer [*sic*] and the James boys joined the forces of Quantrell just before the raid on Lawrence and it was here young Palmer made a record for bravery, daring and loyalty to his commander that stayed with him until his last days. These mere boys took the same part in the raid that older men took and, after they dashed through the town on that memorable day, Palmer was ordered by his chief to retreat and, as he retreated, to burn and kill everything and everybody in sight. Soon heavy firing was heard, hundreds of homes and stores were burning and citizens and farmers who took up whatever kind of weapons they could find were shot down as if their doing so gave the Quantrellites great pleasure. In the midst of this terrible affray, young Palmer was seen going down the street astride his horse at top speed, a blazing six-shooter in each hand, carrying out to the letter the orders of his chief.

If Parmer had any redeeming qualities, it was loyalty, for he remained faithful to Quantrill . . . all the way to his death bed.

ARCHIE CLEMENTS

The sadistic, perhaps mad, mutilator

If Bloody Bill Anderson was a madman, his right-hand man and designated executioner, seventeen-year-old Archie Clements was demonic.

By the time the band had gone to Texas to spend the winter of 1863, "Little" Archie was a veteran at eighteen years of age and devoted to Anderson. A word from his commander and Archie would not only slit a throat or shoot a man who had just surrendered, but he would scalp and mutilate the body of his victim.

Clements was from Kingsville in Johnson County, Missouri. He was small in stature, with blond hair and an evil smile that seemed permanently etched on his face. His eyes, though gray, appeared to change color.

Examples of Clements' disregard for life are abundant. In Carroll County, as Anderson rooted out Federals and killed them, one of the victims cursed him. Clements jumped on the man, a wild grin on his face, and slit his throat with a bowie knife.

After ambushing Federal soldiers of the Seventeenth Illinois on the Huntsville road, Archie scalped two of the victims and Anderson attached a semiliterate note to their bodies: "You come to hunt bush whackers. Now you are skelpt. Clemyent Skept you. Wm. Anderson." Anderson obviously did not write the note, since he was well educated, but the message was his.

In his biography *Complete and Authentic life of Jesse James*, Carl Breihan tells a story of Archie releasing a young Federal soldier, which was a rarity. Later, when Jesse received one of his wounds to the lungs, Breihan states: "Two days later Jesse was found and nursed back to partial health by Arch Clements, the tender-hearted guerrilla who had refused to execute the young Federal soldier in the woods." One wonders if Breihan was being sarcastic or attempting humor in referring to Archie as "tender-hearted."

FLETCHER TAYLOR

The murderer of Sophia Butt's husband?

In 1861, when he first began his reign of terror, Quantrill had only about fifteen men, and one of these was Fletcher "Fletch" Taylor. Taylor came from either Platte County, Wisconsin, or Jackson County, Missouri, depending on which historian's account you want to accept. In *The Life and Times of*

Jesse James, by Carl Breihan, Taylor is shown in a picture with Jesse and Frank James. Frank is dressed in a Confederate uniform. The cutline on the picture reads: "This rare portrait was taken in Nashville, Tennessee, at the close of the Civil War. It shows (left to right) Charles F. (Fletch) Taylor of Platte County, Wisconsin, a member of the Quantrill Guerrillas; Frank James in Confederate uniform showing the three stars on the collar; and Jesse James, not yet 20."

Three stars on Frank's collar would indicate that he was a colonel in the infantry. But is was hard to tell the actual rank of the bushwhackers, since most of the time they wore Federal uniforms taken from victims.

Fletcher headed up small groups of his own raiders from time to time during the war as his relationship with Quantrill varied from trusted scout (Lawrence), to a mistrust that contributed to the dissolving of the guerrillas and the abandonment of Quantrill by most of the raiders in Texas.

Perhaps the relationship would have survived if Fletcher had not called Quantrill's live-in lover, Kate, a whore and if he had not killed a friend of Quantrill's in Texas.

In *Noted Guerrillas,* written by John Edwards in 1877, Fletcher is described as "a low massive Hercules, who, when he had one arm shot off, made the other all the more powerful. Built like a quarter-horse, knowing nature well, seeing equally in darkness and light, rapacious for exercise, having an anatomy like a steam engine, impervious to fatigue like a Cossack, and to hunger like an Apache, he always hunted a fight and always fought for a funeral."

Edwards always had a way of making the bushwhackers look like heros or gods.

DAVID POOLE

A heartless killer

Very little has been written about the early life of David Poole, or why he chose the bushwhacker war. Even his name is in question, as Castel, in both *William Clarke Quantrill* and *Bloody*

Bill Anderson spells it with an "e," while Leslie, Breihan, and Connelley spell it Pool.

Pictures of Poole show a marked contrast. The clean-shaven Poole has a prominent Adam's apple on a long neck, with bushy, almost curly hair draped over his ears and fanning out.

Another photo shows him with a full beard, with the hair and beard running together. But one thing remains the same: the piercing, sad eyes that spoke of the cruelty that lived within but belied the grotesque comic character the surface revealed.

Early in the guerrilla war in Missouri and Kansas, Poole was listed as one of the leaders and rode sometimes with Quantrill, sometimes with Anderson, and at times led his own group of raiders.

At the Lawrence massacre, Poole was listed as a captain, although the guerrillas elected their own officers, probably in an effort to make their depredations appear to be a genuine military operation.

GEORGE TODD

The ditch digger who buried a lot of men

If the Civil War had not come along, George Todd, a stonemason and sometimes ditch digger from Kansas City, would probably have found another excuse for killing people.

After the surrender of Keytesville, Missouri, by Union lieutenant Anthony Pleyer in the fall of 1864, Todd told the soon-to-be-court-martialed officer that he was not a Confederate officer but a bushwhacker and intended to follow bushwhacking as long as he lived.

Like most of the gang, Todd had a story of destruction of home and death of family members to justify his entry into the guerrilla war, but verification is lacking.

According to John N. Edwards, who was personally acquainted with the bushwhacker, Todd was born in Scotland but fled to Canada after killing a man and migrated to Jackson County, Missouri, where he promptly got into trouble with the law. Any story of persecution by the Union authorities was probably invented, like Quantrill's own tale of his brother being killed in Kansas.

The round-faced, blond-headed boy was prime material for the guerrilla band and came to be known as one of the most heartless and ferocious killers who rode with Quantrill.

Todd was one of the early members of Quantrill's gang and remained loyal to the chieftain until the spring of 1864, when, returning to Missouri from Texas, they had a falling-out and Todd rode on to Missouri to organize his own band of Irish guerrillas.

Todd was a murderous killer who looked forward to Lawrence and on the way there killed an old enemy, Joseph Stone, by beating him to death with a gun so there would be no noise.

Quantrill probably did very little killing himself, but at a nod from the leader, Todd the executioner took joy in performing the commands of his colonel.

When the Federals hanged Jim Vaughn, a captured guerrilla, in such a sloppy way that it took fifteen minutes for him to die at the end of the rope, Todd rode in revenge on June 17, 1863, just south of Westport, where he and his gang ambushed a Federal column and killed fourteen troopers. Those who were only wounded were executed where they lay, and on a piece of paper between the teeth of one of them, Todd left the message "Remember the dying words of Jim Vaughn."

COLE YOUNGER

Forced into a life of crime?

Henry Younger was a successful farmer and stock raiser in Jackson County, and, according to Richard Brownlee, he was a strong Union supporter and against Missouri seceding.[6] But when Jayhawkers took his wagons and carriages, along with forty saddle horses and his stock of whiskey, his politics changed.

He was murdered by a Captain Walley[7] of the Fifth Missouri Militia Cavalry, and soon afterward, his home was burned and his family left without shelter in the cold Missouri winter.

Coleman Younger, the eldest son of Henry, had already been

associated with Quantrill when his father was killed, and the murder drove him into the brush as a full-time bushwhacker.

Breihan, in his book *Younger Brothers,* related the story of seventeen-year-old Cole, who was helping his dad deliver mail, coming across a hanging in the woods and being shot at by Quantrill as he ran from the scene. The shot was only a warning, and Quantrill let the Missouri lad go home.

The Younger family were not poor farmers as were so many of the raiders' families, but the unionists still gave Cole, James, Bob, and John good reason to hate them.

> Headquarters Central District Of Missouri
> Jefferson City, Mo., January 27, 1863
> Maj. Gen. Samuel R. Curtis:
> In several counties in the district no courts of record of any kind have held a session for several terms past, say, for more than eighteen months. The records have been stolen, perhaps destroyed, and the civil officers driven from the country. Recently I arrested a Captain Walley, who had murdered one Harry [*sic*] Younger, in Jackson County, for his money. The evidence of his guilt was so clear and conclusive that he confessed it. Preferring that he should be regularly tried and punished, I directed a court to be held in Independence for that purpose. The witnesses, soldiers in the Fifth Regiment Missouri State Militia, who were stationed in Harrisonville, in Cass County were sent to attend court. When on their way, they were bushwhacked by a band under Bird [*sic*][8] Younger, a son of the murdered man, and the court was not held.
> Ben Loan
> Brigadier General, Missouri State Militia[9]

"The fact that my father was killed in cold blood filled my heart with a lust for vengeance," said Younger. He had vowed while staring into the face of his dead father, but Cole, like Bill Anderson, was to receive another reason for hating Yankees. Captain Walley, his old enemy, had arrested two of his cousins, Charity Kerr and Nannie Harris, and three of Cole's sisters. They were imprisoned in the infamous "jail" in Kansas City that collapsed. Charity was killed, but his sisters and Nannie escaped serious injury.

When the tall, broad-shouldered young man had joined the Quantrill band in 1862, he was just eighteen years old.

WILLIAM GREGG

One of the first to join Quantrill

Bill Gregg, along with George Todd, Joe Vaughn, Bill Hallar, John and Jim Little, Ed and John Koger, Harrison Trace, and Joe Gilchrist, were the original members of the Quantrill gang.

William Gregg claimed that one day he had been standing by while Union men burned Mrs. Crawford's house. When two of the Union men had "snatched a lace cap from her head and threw it into the flames of the burning building," Gregg had disregarded all danger, whipped out his pistols, and killed both men. Defense of womankind was Gregg's retrospective justification for having acted as a killer. This was a typically personal category for explaining revenge, extended to include all women, all of whom, to Gregg, had resembled his mother.[10]

The guerrillas typically defended women, except for prostitutes and black women, whom most of them treated with disdain or used for sexual release.

In August of 1862, Quantrill, along with his men, were supposedly sworn in to the Confederate army at Morgan Walker's farm by Col. Gideon W. Thompson, and Gregg was listed as third lieutenant. The legality of the swearing-in is questionable, and whether or not the guerrillas were members of the Confederate army is a matter that has been debated by historians ever since.

At the Battles of Cane Hill and Prairie Grove, Arkansas, it was reported that Gregg was in command of the guerrillas, who fought with Gen. Jo Shelby's forces.

According to Gregg, in the manuscript he wrote entitled *A Little Dab Of History without Embellishment,* his purpose at the Lawrence massacre was to get money to help the destitute Southern families of the border counties in Missouri, and to this end he galloped down Massachusetts Street during the height of the raid with Quantrill, shooting from side to side, and robbed all the guests at the hotel. Gregg said later that Quantrill's men "went to Lawrence with hell in their necks, and raised hell after they got there." At Baxter Springs, Gregg led the charge on Fort Blair.

Perhaps part of the reason for Gregg's entry into guerrilla warfare is best noted by his wife, who in her memoirs wrote that Federal soldiers had come to her childhood home, forced her family slaves to go to Kansas, and placed her father in jail several times for abetting Southern sympathizers and refugees of General Order No. 11. However, that order was not issued until Gregg had ridden with Quantrill for about two years.

Like other bushwhackers who wrote memoirs after the war, Gregg tried to soften his involvement with the atrocities that occurred. He saw himself as the defender of the downtrodden and of womanhood after the depredations of the Union soldiers on the people of Missouri.

JOHN THRAILKILL

The conqueror of Keyteville

There is nothing to confirm the early life of John Thrailkill, or what drove him into bushwhacking.

He led his own band of cutthroats north of the Missouri River for a time, and after the breakup of the guerrillas he rode mostly with Todd and was primarily responsible for the surrender of Keyteville, Missouri, which happened to be Sterling Price's hometown.

KATE (KING) CLARKE

Quantrill's teenage queen

She was not even thirteen years old when she met Bill Quantrill and was to later state that she fell in love with him the first time she saw him.

Because of her age, her parents objected to the romance

from the start, but when she turned thirteen, she either eloped with Quantrill or was carried off by him, depending on which historian you want to believe. Marriage at that age in those times was not uncommon. Whether or not they were actually married is up for debate, too, but they supposedly were wedded at a little church near her home in Jackson County.

There were reports that Kate, dressed in men's clothing, often rode with the men, but that is probably not true, although she may have done so when they were changing locations. She was an excellent horsewoman.

At any rate, the little thirteen-year-old girl was to grow into a beautiful woman who experienced the agony of widowhood at a very early age. One has to speculate as to what her life would have been like had she not met the violet-eyed charmer from Ohio.

WILLIAM CLARKE QUANTRILL

The violet-eyed mastermind

Dick Hopson moved to Sherman, Texas, in 1861 and was editor of the *Sherman Courier*. He reported he knew Quantrill personally. According to Hopson, "Quantrill was below medium height at 5'8", of sandy complexion, with sandy hair and blue eyes that seemed to turn to violet at times. He was quiet, unassuming, never raised his voice in conversation, never smoked, drank, or swore. While there were about fifty or sixty men with him in Sherman, all of them were under perfect discipline. He never spoke to a man but one time in a low tone of voice, and no man was ever known to disobey him."

Apparently Hopson never saw the Quantrill who ordered the killing of hundreds of innocents, or the Quantrill who faked his past to create an excuse for barbarism.

William Clarke Quantrill was born at Canal Dover, Ohio, on July 31, 1837, the oldest of twelve children. Even as a youngster, he began to expose the cruel underside of his character.

William Gregg described him much as Hopson did, adding that the cold blue, sometimes violet, eyes, stared out from beneath "heavy upper lids that gave his face an almost Mongol appearance." Behind those cold eyes was a charismatic mastermind.

John Connelley stated that very little is known of Quantrill's childhood, then went on to report: "He was solitary, wandering in the woods with firearms when quite young. There he shot small game and maimed domestic animals for amusement. He would often nail a snake to a tree and let it remain there in torture until it died. He carried small snakes in his pockets, and these he would throw on his sister and other girls at school and laugh heartily at their terror. He would stick a knife into a cow by the roadside, or stab a horse. He often tortured dogs and cats to enjoy their cries of distress." [11]

He once locked a girl up in the bell tower of a church and went off and left her there.

He became a teacher at sixteen, and after teaching in his hometown of Canal Dover for two years, he moved to Mendota, Illinois, and then to Fort Wayne, Indiana. Interestingly, Fort Wayne was the former home of Sophia Suttenfield, whose life would intersect with Quantrill's in Texas. It was reported that the last move was because he had killed a man in Illinois, but no charges were ever made.

He migrated to Kansas in 1857, when the border wars were just warming up. In 1858, he went to Salt Lake City but returned to Lawrence, Kansas, in the summer of 1859 and taught at a school near Osatatomie. He quit the school after the end of the term and hung around Lawrence abolitionists.

It was rumored he practiced horse stealing, and without a doubt, he joined in the taking of slaves from owners in Missouri. On one such raid, on the farm of Morgan Walker, Quantrill turned traitor on his abolitionist friends and reported the affair to Walker, who gathered at his ranch to await the slave thieves.

Quantrill led his friends to the farm, then got out of the line of fire while Walker's son, Andy, and his friends shot into the raiders, killing one, wounding two, and sending the others running for Lawrence. One of the men returned to help a wounded comrade and managed to get him away from the Walker farm, but they were later killed by Walker and Quantrill.

The story was reported in the Kansas City papers, and

Quantrill found himself in much favor with the slaveholders of Jackson County. Perhaps it was at that time the cruel young man from Ohio ceased to be a Yankee and adopted the Southern cause.

It is doubtful, however, that Quantrill ever really cared anything about the South or slavery. His heart was filled with revenge and personal gain, and probably a very large ego that drove him toward fame, or infamy.

He invented a story about a brother who was killed by Jayhawkers, and he joined Montgomery's Jayhawkers under the name of Charley Hart. He claimed to have killed, one by one, the men who were responsible for his brother's death while pretending to be one of them.

In the years ahead, his followers would believe the story of his brother's death, as most of them had tales to tell of family being harmed by unionists. Obviously, Quantrill invented the story so he would have that common denominator with the other Missourians.

He rode with Andy Walker for a time and killed a man who had struck a woman with a gun. Soon his leadership skills began to surface and he formed his own band of bushwhackers, ten men who had a reason to hate the Union because of the mistreatment of their families. Quantrill must have told the story of his brother's murder around many a campfire.

His first engagement, according to official records, was near Blue Springs in early February 1862, and Capt. William S. Oliver was determined to put an early end to his career as a guerrilla:

> Headquarters Camp Stevenson
> Independence, February 3, 1862
> General: I have just returned from an expedition which I was compelled to undertake in search of the notorious Quantrill and his gang of robbers in the vicinity of Blue Springs. Without mounted men at my disposal, despite numerous applications to various points, I have seen this infamous scoundrel rob mails, steal the coaches and horses, and commit other similar outrages upon society even within sight of this city. Mounted on the best horses of the country, he has defied pursuit, making his camp in the bottoms of the ——— and the Blue, and roving over a circuit of 30 miles. I mounted

a company of my command and went to Blue Springs. The first night there myself, with 5 men, were ambushed by him and fired upon. We killed 2 of his men (of which he had 18 or 20) and wounded a third. The next day, we killed 1 more of the worst of the gang, and before we left succeeded in dispersing them. I obtained 6 or 7 wagons of pork and a quantity of tobacco, hidden and preserved for the use of the Southern army, and recovered also the valuable stage-coach, with 2 of their horses. I was absent for a week, and can say that no men were ever more earnest or subject to greater privations and hardships than both the mounted men and the infantry I employed on this expedition.

Quantrill will not leave this section unless he is chastised and driven from it. I hear of him tonight 15 miles from here, with new recruits, committing outrages on Union men, a large body of whom have come in tonight, driven out by him. Families of Union men are coming into the city to-night asking of me escorts to bring in their goods and chattels, which I duly furnished.[12]

Soon after this, young men, surprisingly young, began to join the Quantrill guerrillas. Teenagers like Jesse James, Allen Parmer, and William Gregg would come to serve in the irregular brush army. Most of these men had legitimate reasons to take revenge on Union troops, but Quantrill, who had tremendous leadership abilities and, unlike many of his followers, an education, took their hatred and vows of revenge and turned them to meet his own vengeful and cruel desires.

After the guerrillas' women were killed or injured in the Kansas City jail collapse, Quantrill fanned the flames of hatred and led the half-maddened guerrillas on the Lawrence, Kansas, raid.

Lawrence, which had rejected Quantrill, would go down in history as the epitome of massacres and needless murder. There was, of course, the black-flag policy, which neither asked for nor gave quarter, but those killed at Lawrence were not military men, although some of them had ridden with the Jayhawkers.

The "battle" of Lawrence was to be the high-water mark for Quantrill, for it stirred the Federals into a frenzy of activity aimed at eradication of the bushwhackers on the western border of Missouri. Hardly had the bodies of the Lawrence victims grown cold when Thomas Ewing issued Order No. 11, which

This 1870 painting by George Caleb Bingham depicts the agony of Order No. 11, which was one of the factors that led to Quantrill's exodus to Texas in the fall of 1863.

—Courtesy of the State Historical Society of Missouri

caused great suffering to the people who supported the South and lived on the Missouri-Kansas border.

The Lawrence raid also raised eyebrows among the Southern leadership in regard to Quantrill's methods of fighting a war.

When the fall of 1863 came, most of their comfort stations from Southern sympathizers had been erased by Order No. 11, and with the falling of leaves, most of their cover in the Sni Hills disappeared as well, and so Quantrill led his band south to the safety and warmth of Texas. It was to be the beginning of a harsh winter, however.

Before they got out of Kansas, however, there was to be one more slaying of innocents. Not even aware that there were troops at Baxter Springs in a little mud fort called Blair, Quantrill's men found it by accident and attacked.

At that moment, the bushwhackers' old nemesis, Gen. James Blunt, arrived with a wagon train and his own brass band. Blunt escaped, but his troops were shot, even after many of them put down their weapons and surrendered. The band was wiped out, including a twelve-year-old drummer boy.

Finally, in Texas, Quantrill thought he could relax and enjoy the comforts of some of the plantation owners, who looked on him as a celebrity, but problems with his own leaders and with the commander of the Northeast District of Texas were to lead to more trouble than even the wiry and clever Quantrill could cope with.

Military Personnel: Blue and Gray

The events that were about to unfold in the little city of Sherman, Texas, Grayson County, and northeast Texas involved both Union and Confederate officers. Each played a role, mostly unwittingly, in the historical events that divided and changed the guerrilla band of Quantrill.

It may be a stretch of the imagination to call them historical events, for the results had no bearing whatsoever on the outcome of the war but played an important part of the "war within the war."

There had never been a war like the American Civil War, and all their West Point training could not prepare the officers to deal with brushmen, Indians, and the infidelity of their own soldiers.

Although Texas was considered the granary of the South, the military men found themselves understaffed and undersupplied, for the leadership of the South knew the war would be, for the most part, fought and won in the eastern battlefields.

The Northern commanders in Missouri were not prepared, with all their equipment and supplies, to deal with a populace that operated in small groups of snipers and fought as if they didn't care if they lived or died, and civilians who were anxious to risk life and limb to supply and hide them.

This was not a stand-up war, with opposing armies marching in neat ranks and firing at each other at close range. It was a conflict where you died in the dark with a slit throat or were hanged from a tree with hemp or hickory bark around your neck.

JAMES BLUNT

A radical abolitionist

A stubby bulldog of a man with dark, sunken eyes, a bushy moustache, and a tiny goatee hanging on the bottom of his lower lip, Blunt was born in Maine and received a medical degree in Ohio. But after moving to Kansas he began helping the madman John Brown smuggle escaped slaves into Canada.

When the war broke out, he commanded a cavalry regiment under James Lane of the Kansas Brigade. When it was called into regular Union service in April of 1862, Blunt was promoted to brigadier general. That fall he defeated Confederate Indian forces at Old Fort Wayne and accomplished victories at Cane Hill and Prairie Grove in spite of some nervousness that led to admitted mistakes.

He served as commander of the Army of the Frontier but is best remembered for two things: his fanatic and religious enforcement of the black-flag order, which stated that guerrillas were not regular Confederate soldiers and were to be executed when captured as criminals, and his defeat by Quantrill at Baxter Springs, an event that led to him being relieved of his command, although he was reassigned by President Lincoln to recruit blacks for the Union army.

His enforcement of the black-flag order, and particularly the hanging of bushwhacker Jimmy Vaughan, only enraged the guerrillas and led to more needless killing.

On January 23, 1862, Gen. H. W. Halleck, the commanding officer of the district that included Missouri, wrote his adversary, Gen. Sterling Price of the Confederate army:

> . . .You must be aware, general, that no orders of yours can save from punishment spies, marauders, robbers, incendiaries, guerrilla bands, &c., who violate the laws of war. You cannot give immunity to crime. But let us fully understand each other on this point. If you send armed forces, wearing the garb of soldiers and duly organized and enrolled as legitimate belligerent, to destroy rail roads, bridges, &c., as a military act, we shall kill them, if possible, in open warfare, or, if we capture them, we shall treat them as prisoners of war.
>
> But it is well understood that you have sent numbers of your adherents in the garb of peaceful citizens, and under false pretenses, through our lines into Northern Missouri, to rob and destroy the property of Union men and to burn and destroy railroad bridges, thus endangering the lives of thousands, and this, too, without any military necessity or possible military advantage. Moreover, peaceful citizens of Missouri, quietly working on their farms, have been instigated by your emissaries to take up arms as insurgents, and to rob and plunder and to commit arson and murder. They do not even act under the garb of soldiers, but under false pretenses that men guilty of such crimes, although especially appointed by you, are entitled to the rights and immunities of ordinary prisoners of war . . . I shall, whenever I can, punish such crimes, by whomsoever they may be committed.[13]

Blunt took his responsibility to carry out these orders by Halleck very seriously, and, as in the case of Vaughn, turned the executions into a public spectacle in hopes of deterring other rebels. It didn't work.

THOMAS EWING

The most hated Union officer

Probably no other Federal officer epitomized evil and cruelty to the Bushwhackers more than Gen. Thomas Ewing Jr., the author (with President Lincoln's approval, and with the help of Kansas senator James Lane) of General Order No. 11, which imposed so much suffering on the people of the western Missouri border counties that leaned toward the Southern cause.

Ewing's family was a prominent one in Ohio before the war, and Thomas served as the personal secretary to President Zachary Taylor in 1848. His father had served as secretary of the interior. William Tecumseh Sherman, the general who burned a path across the South during the war, was raised in the Ewing household after the death of his father in 1829, the year Thomas was born. Sherman even took Ewing's sister, Ellen, as a bride. The burning of homes in Missouri under Ewing's Order No. 11 and Sherman's devastation in the South led historian Thomas Goodrich to wonder if their father allowed them to play with matches when they were young. Ewing's brother, Hugh, also became a Union general.

Thomas attended Brown University, and after getting a degree in law in Cincinnati he moved to Kansas in 1856 to practice his trade, becoming involved in the effort to bring Kansas into the Union as an free state. He also served as Kansas' first Supreme Court chief justice.

In 1862 he joined the army as a colonel and worked as a recruiter for a time, but after leading the troops at the Battles of Cane Hill and Prairie Grove, he was promoted to brigadier general on March 13, 1863.

STERLING PRICE

The Robert E. Lee of the West

A former governor of the state of Missouri and a tobacco planter and slave owner, Sterling Price was a man torn between loyalties.

He was born on September 20, 1809, at Prince Edward City, Virginia, and came to Missouri at the age of twenty-one with his family. He served as the military governor of New Mexico and was appointed brigadier general.

On returning to Missouri, he served as a legislator in the early 1840s and a congressman from 1844 to 1846. He was elected governor in 1852.

At the outbreak of the War between the States, Price at first opposed secession for Missouri, but when then-governor Francis Blair took over Camp Jackson at St. Louis, he tossed his talents into the rebel ring, fought at Wilson's Creek and captured the Union garrison at Lexington.

On March 6, 1862, he was promoted to major general and was at the Battle of Pea Ridge when Ben McCulloch, Henry's brother, was killed.

He led troops at the Battles of Iuka, Corinth, and Helena during the years of 1862 and 1863, but returned to his home state late in the war to lead the doomed expedition to free Missouri and take pressure off the Confederate troops in the besieged East.

"Old Pap," as he was called by his men, was torn between fighting an honorable and "civilized" war, and adopting the bushwhacker method, which seemed to add up to more dead Yankees, at least in the Western theater.

EDMUND KIRBY SMITH

The Christian with rose-colored glasses

Kirby Smith was born in St. Augustine, Florida, on May 16, 1824. He graduated twenty-fifth in his West Point class of 1845 and soon was fighting in the Mexican war, where he was cited for bravery at Cerro Gordo.

By 1855, he had been made a captain in the Second Cavalry Regiment, and when Florida seceded from the Union in 1861, he was commissioned a brigadier general in the Confederate army.

His forces helped turn the tide at the first Battle of Bull Run, where he was wounded. After leading an excursion into

Kentucky, he was named in October 1862 as the commander of the Trans-Mississippi Department, where he spent the remainder of the war.

The black-bearded soldier with the receding hairline (which he enhanced by allowing his hair to grow long in the back) was a dedicated Christian and almost left his command in the fall of 1863 to enter the ministry. Interestingly enough, at that same time, he was having trouble with Quantrill's men in north Texas.

HENRY McCULLOCH

The beleaguered commander of north Texas

Like so many others from Tennessee, Henry Eustace McCulloch moved to Texas. He settled in Guadalupe City, where he served as sheriff, in addition to his farming enterprise.

He served during the Mexican war in the Texas Rangers but for the most part fought Indians. He served in the state legislature and the Senate after the war and in the late 1850s became a U.S. marshall.

Unlike his fellow Tennessean Sam Houston, McCulloch favored secession for Texas when the Civil War became a reality and joined the First Texas Mounted Rifles as a colonel. His brother, Ben, was killed at the Battle of Pea Ridge.

He spent most of his military career within Texas boundaries, except for one engagement at Vicksburg in a failed effort to relieve the siege of the city by Ulysses S. Grant.

As commander of the Northeastern District of Texas in 1863, he became involved (and disgusted) with the guerrillas at Sherman, disapproving of their methods of warfare as well as their personal habits.

JAMES BOURLAND

The hangman of Texas, or Texas hero?

James G. Bourland was born in South Carolina in 1801 and

in 1822 married Catherine Wells in Kentucky. The couple had six children.

In 1840 he moved to Texas and worked as a surveyor. He was the owner of one slave and in 1842 was one of the signers of the Indian treaty. In 1843, he was a lieutenant colonel in the Red River Volunteers and later served in the legislature of the Republic of Texas.

In 1846 he helped raise troops to fight in the Mexican war, but by 1856 it seemed his fighting days were over, as he operated a family store at Bourland Bend in Cooke County.

But in 1859, Governor Hardin Runnels called on Bourland to raise a company of men to put down raids on the citizens by Indians and undesirables. The campaign lasted for six months, and though it failed to destroy the marauding Indians, it did curtail the raids. Bourland, however, gained a reputation for being ruthless.[14]

In 1860 he was listed on the tax rolls as a farmer, but his fortunes had grown. He had $56,260 in real estate and personal property, including twenty-three slaves, and by 1862 he owned land in Cooke, Clay, Hunt, Fannin, Montague, and Wise counties.

In 1861, at the age of sixty, he again became the colonel of a regiment, this time Confederate, and served mostly in the northeast section of Texas throughout the war.

His expertise in Indian affairs became a valuable asset to the Confederacy, as he was able to enlist the services of the Choctaws and Chickasaws.

He is best known for his participation in the great hanging that took place in Gainesville, where he served as the provost marshall. It earned him the nickname "The Hangman of Texas," which is unfortunate, since he could have been remembered as a patriot of Texas, having defended the state against Indians, Mexicans, and Yankees.

PART II

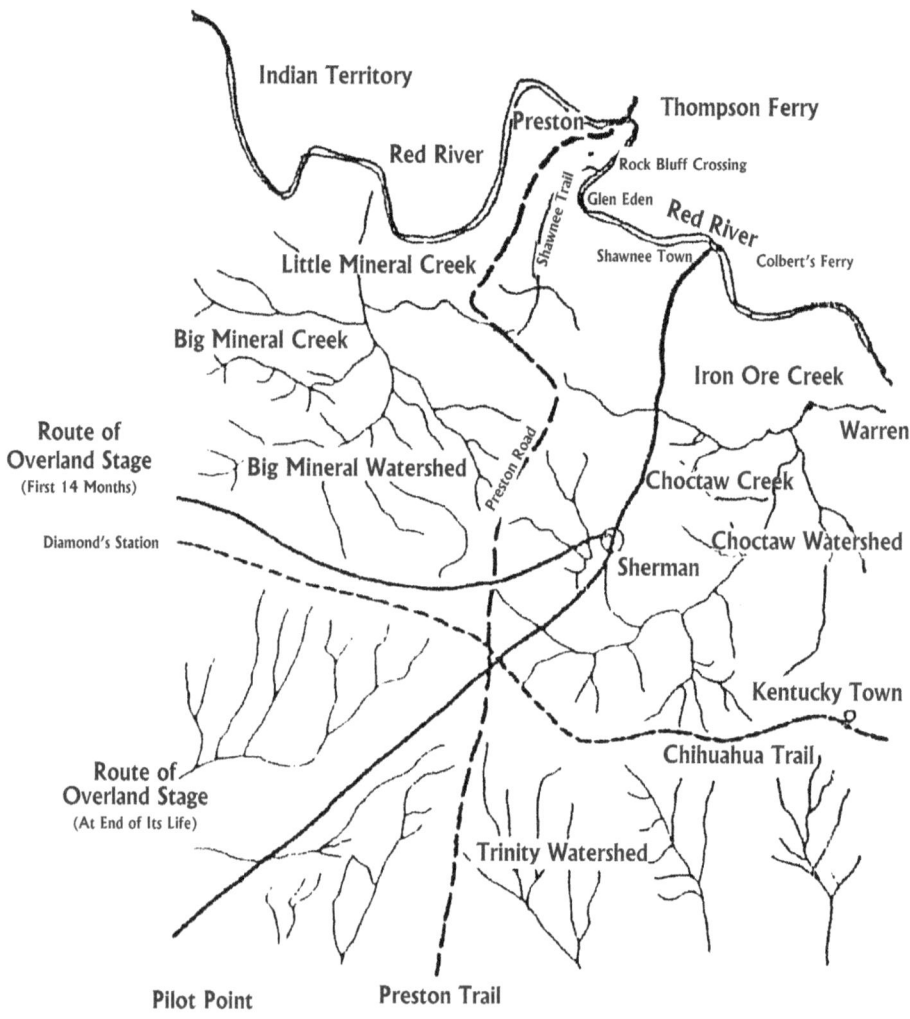

Grayson County, 1848–61.

—Courtesy the Red River Historical Museum

CHAPTER 4

Sherman and Grayson County

The wild frontier that was to become Grayson County was the home of Indians, including the Comanche, Cherokee, and Creek tribes. In the winter, herds of buffalo came south, followed by great packs of wolves.

The area that became Grayson County comprised 942 square miles, divided in twain by separate elevations. The upper level to the west was enclosed by the forest along the Red River to the north and the ribbonlike strip of woods known as Cross Timbers in the west.

In 1778 de Mézières wrote: "From the Brazos River until one reaches Red River, one sees a forest which the natives call Monte Grande. It is very dense but not very wide. It seems to be there for a guide."

And Marcy, who explored the Red River, described the land: "It seems to have been designed as a natural barrier between the civilized man and the savage. As to the east side, there are many springs and brooks. Flowers over a highly prolific soil, with good timber and rank vegetation, teeming with a delightful perfume of flowers of most brilliant hues, interspersed with verdant glades and small prairies, and the most beautiful meadows imaginable. West of the timbers be the prairies and the plains country."

Choctaw Creek was to the east with its valleys and timber, while the marshes of the headwaters of the Sabine and Sulphur rivers and the East Fork of the Trinity were to the south and east.

The land was home to the agricultural Indian tribes of the Caddo Confederacy before the white man came. The tribes included Keechees, Ionies, and Tonkawas. They raised beans, maize, and tobacco.

Besides the buffalo and the wolves, which were seasonal visitors, the land was occupied by herds of wild horses and mustangs, an inheritance from the Spanish explorers. There were also Mexican cougars and panthers, along with a variety of smaller animals such as foxes, raccoons, jackrabbits, snakes, lizards, and of course a multitude of horned toads.

The Indians' food supply was enhanced with wild turkey, sage hens, and prairie chickens, while overhead bald eagles, vultures, and hawks soared. Other birds included a variety of owls, along with woodpeckers, blue jays, mockingbirds, thrushes, orioles, and hummingbirds during migration. At night the sound of the whippoorwill could be heard, and in the fall, thousands of geese veed overhead on their way south for the winter.

Underfoot, a virtual garden of color graced the earth with brilliant colors. Indian blankets and red splashes of paintbrush, along with buffalo bean, lupines, toad flax, squaw weed, dogtooth violet, wood violet, beardtongue, and rattlesnake flowers filled the fields with color and aroma.

There was also an abundance of wild plum, dogwood, and redbud, along with Texas plum, asters, button bushes, coreopsis, butterfly bushes, and phlox.

The woods were filled with native pecans, hickory, and Texas chinaberry. The snarled and hardened bois d'arc trees were plentiful, their green "horse apples" littering the ground beneath them. There were haws with berries, and stretch berry vines. Blackberries and wild strawberries abounded. On the prairies, the native grama grasses were as high as a bison's hump.

The ground had been traversed by both Spanish and French explorers, and migrant trappers entered, leaving only footprints as they returned to Fort Smith, Arkansas, and civilization.

No effort was made to inhabit the wilderness until John Hart, the first known English-speaking pioneer, crossed the Red River and established the first outpost at Preston Bend.

Hart had served in the Texas revolution before returning to

his occupation of trapper and Indian trader, operating out of Fort Smith. But in 1837, he returned to Texas and staked a claim, along with partners James and William Baker, at the mouth of the Washita River. They cleared about seventeen acres of the virgin woods and built three log cabins, where the partnership continued until 1839.

Hart served as the sheriff of Fannin County (Grayson had not yet been established) but was killed in 1840, or perhaps 1841, by a partner of Holland Coffee, who had occupied part of Hart's land.

Very little is known of Coffee's background, except that, like Hart, he was an Indian trader and had operated a trading post on the Red River just west of Cross Timbers in 1833. He was accused of trading whiskey and guns to Indians in exchange for horses and cattle that had been stolen from white settlers but was never convicted of any crime.

In spite of his business reputation, the people elected him in 1838 to the Third Congress as a representative, and along the way, by hook or crook, he accumulated six sections of land.

He spoke several languages and had been instrumental in negotiating treaties with the Indians.

The colonel received some land grants for his war service and opened a trading post at what was then called Coffee Bend, but in 1840, a fort was established and the place became known as Preston Bend, after the commanding captain, William Preston.

Civilization was making inroads into northeast Texas and in 1841 the first newspaper, the *Northern Standard*, was printed in Clarksville, and in Sherman the first courthouse was built at a cost of $232; a big barbecue and dance was held to celebrate the occasion.

Another prosperous settler was Col. John Potts, who moved to north Texas with his 100 slaves and established a large plantation near the Preston Bend community. Like Sophia Suttenfield Auginbaugh Holland Butt Porter, he was to play a part in the Missouri guerrillas' escapades.

CHAPTER 5

Mineral Creek

And so, the stage was set for the final performance of the Missouri guerrillas before they were to splinter into opposing forces. There would be at least one more curtain call back home in Missouri, but for the most part, the guerrilla band was to dissolve into weakened segments while they were in Texas.

All the actors were moving into place, from the migrant killers and thieves from Missouri to the honest and not-so-honest citizens of Grayson County. Each was to play a part, whether a minor or major role, in the events that took place in the fall of 1863 and the winter and spring of 1864 and have an impact on the history of northeast Texas and the nation.

Franklin Colbert had fought off a challenge from M. A. McBride to keep his rights to operate the ferry across the Red River by obtaining McBride's land on the Texas side of the stream, but the unpredictability of the flat, red-banked waterway was always a challenge. Low water meant riders could cross without paying, while flood level could wipe out your business in a wall of churning red mud.[1]

In 1860, Colbert had seen an increase in traffic into Texas and had noticed a deterioration in the quality of the pilgrims. Hard men from the border states who had lost all they owned and even some family members were looking for a fresh start in the promised land of Texas.

In 1862, although he was probably unaware of it, Colbert may have ferried William Clarke Quantrill across the muddy Red and then back again as the retired schoolteacher about to turn guerrilla made a trip to Texas. Actually, Quantrill had been to Texas as early as 1859, probably still hoping to claim a piece of the state. Quantrill's relationship with John Hart could be questioned, but it is interesting to note that when he needed an alias, Quantrill used the name Charley Hart. His visit was short, however, and he quickly crossed back over to Indian Territory, where he made friends and connections that were to become valuable later.

When Quantrill rode to Texas in the winter of 1862, he had not yet attained his apex of notoriety, and the ferryman probably figured it was just another bunch of Missouri riff-raff. Quantrill's 1862 visit was a brief one, for he was in Little Rock on December 7.

An 1863 crossing was different. The ferryman at Colbert's Ferry looked at the motley crew approaching his landing and could probably tell from the fit of their blue uniforms and their unmilitary movement that they were not Union soldiers.

But one thing he did know was that with this crowd, he would walk the cable and propel the flat-bottomed boat across the river as quickly as possible, and without conversation. He had learned that it did not pay to whistle "Dixie" or hum "The Battle Hymn of the Republic." It was wise to not even make eye contact with most of his customers.

He also knew that his fee might not be paid, but he would not push the point, lest he find himself out of the ferryboat business and looking at the red soil of Oklahoma from the bottom side up.

There is the possibility, if the river was low enough, that the bushwhackers forded the Red and avoided the ferry.

From Baxter Springs, it had not been a good trip for the bushwhackers. They had left behind six dead white soldiers and one black soldier at Fort Blair, and counting General Blunt's band and drummer boy, the total dead was ninety-eight. That count also included Jack Mann, the negro who was to meet his fate on the road to Texas.

At the fort, ten whites and thirteen blacks were wounded,

along with the woman and child who were shot (intentionally, according to reports). Lieutenant Pond reported the bushwhacker casualties to be much heavier.

They had buried their comrade, William Bledshoe, along with the captured negro Jack Mann, who was shot after he dug two shallow graves, one for Bledsoe, and one for himself.

When they reached Gen. Douglas Cooper's camp on the Canadian River on October 12, Quantrill gave his men a rest and wrote his report on his recent activities to Sterling Price. Quantrill's report to Price was to bring a flurry of correspondence from the hierarchy of the Confederates in Texas:

> Report of Col. W. C. Quantrill, Confederate Service
> In Camp on Canadian
> October 13, 1863
> I have the honor to make the following report of my march from the Missouri River to the Canadian, a distance of 450 miles.
> I started on the morning of October 2, at daybreak, and had an uninterrupted march until night, and encamped on Grand River for three hours; then marched to the Osage. We continued the march from day to day, taking a due southwest course, leaving Carthage 12 miles east, crossing Shoal Creek at the falls, then going due west into the Seneca Nation.
> On October 6, about 2 p.m., the advance reported a train ahead. I ordered the advance to press on and ascertain the nature of it. Captain Brinker being in command of the advance, he soon discovered an encampment, which he supposed to be the camp of the train; in this we were mistaken. It proved to be the camp belonging to Fort Baxter [*sic*], recently built and garrisoned with negroes, 45 miles south of Fort Scott, Kans. When the advance came near the camp they saw that they were not discovered, and they fell back a short distance to wait for the command to come up. I now ordered the column to close in and to form by fours and charge, and leading the head of the column myself with Captains Brinker and Pool, took about one-half of the column to the encampment which they had discovered, still being ignorant of the fort. This they charged, driving everything before them, and in two minutes were in possession of the fort. The negroes took shelter behind their quarters. Having no support, my men were compelled to fall

back. Not knowing myself where the fort was, I moved with three companies—Captains Todd, Estes, and Garrett, in all 150 men—out on the prairie north of the camp, and discovered a train with 125 men as an escort, which proved to be Major-General (J.G) Blunt and staff with a body guard and headquarters train, moving headquarters from Fort Scott, Kans., to Fort Smith, Ark. I immediately drew up in line of battle, and at this time I heard heavy firing on my left, and on finding out discovered, for the first time, the fort, with at least half of my men engaged there. I ordered them to join me immediately, which they did, on the double quick. General Blunt formed his escort, still in doubt as to who we were. I formed 250 men of all the companies and ordered a charge. Up to this time not a shot had been fired, nor until we were within 60 yards of them, when they gave us a volley too high to hurt anyone, and then fled in the wildest confusion on the prairie. We soon closed up on them, making fearful havoc on every side. We continued to chase about 4 miles, when I called the men off, only leaving about 40 of them alive. On returning, we found they had left us 9 six-mule wagons, well leaded; 1 buggy (General Blunt's), 1 fine ambulance; 1 fine brass band and wagon, fully rigged.

Among the killed were General Blunt, Majors Curtis, Sinclair, and (B. S.) Henning, Captain Tufft (Tough), and 3 lieutenants of the staff, and about 80 privates of the escort. My loss here was 1 man killed (William Bledshoe) and 8 severely wounded (John Koger). In the charge on the fort my loss was 2 men killed (Robert Ward and William Lotspeach); wounded, Lieutenant Toothman and Private Thomas Hill. Federal loss at the fort, 1 lieutcnant and 15 privates killed; number wounded, not known.

We have the trophies two stand of colors, General Blunt's sword, his commission (brigadier-general and major-general, all his official papers &c., belonging to headquarters. After taking what we wanted from the train; we destroyed it, fearing we could not carry it away in the face of so large a force. We then sent a flag of truce to the fort to see if we had any wounded there. There was none.

I did not think it prudent to attack the fort again, and as we had wounded men already to carry, and it was so far to bring them (I concluded) that I would leave the fort. So at 5 p.m. I took up the line of march due south on the old Texas road. We

marched 15 miles, and encamped for the night. From this
place to the Canadian River we caught about 150 Federal
Indians and negroes in the Nation gathering ponies. We
brought none of them through.

We arrived at General (D. H.) Cooper's camp on the 12th
in good health and condition.

At some future day I will send you a complete report of my
summer's campaign on the Missouri River.

Your obedient servant, W. C. Quantrill,
Colonel Commanding, &c. Insert[2]

After refusing Anderson's request to attack the fort,
Quantrill sent Todd in under a flag of truce to demand a surrender, but it was refused by Lieutenant Pond. Todd then in-
quired as to the status of prisoners, and Pond in his report alluded to the fact that Todd had come to the fort under a flag of
truce and lied about his own casualties and even told Pond that
Major Curtis was a wounded prisoner, when he was, in fact, already dead. Pond, however could tell that Todd was lying:

> I answered that I had taken no prisoners; that I had wounded
> several of his men, whom I had seen fall from their horses, and
> would see that they were cared for, provided he would do the
> same by our men. He said he had 12 privates and the adjutant-
> general (Major Curtis) prisoners, and that I had killed about
> 50 of his men, and if I would promise to take care of his
> wounded, and see that they were paroled after they were able
> to leave, he would promise me that no harm should befall
> Curtis or our men. This, I think, was intended for a blind to
> find out what I had done, as they had already murdered Major
> Curtis and all the prisoners.[3]

Although a young man, Pond had learned not to believe or trust
a bushwhacker.

When Sterling Price heard of the attack, he had his assistant
adjutant general write to Quantrill, with instructions to write a
complete report and to be sure to list all the Union atrocities so
that in the eyes of the world, Lawrence and Baxter Springs
would be justified. It would seem that Price wanted to avoid

dealing with the unmilitary actions of Quantrill as much as possible and assigned the task of answering the report to a subordinate:

Headquarters Price's Division
Camp Bragg, Ark. Nov. 2, 1863
Col. William C. Quantrill, Commanding Calvary:
   Colonel: I am desired by Major-General Price to acknowledge the receipt of your report of your march from the Missouri River to the Canadian, and that he takes pleasure in congratulating you and your gallant command upon the success attending it. General Price is very anxious that you prepare the report of your summer campaign, alluded to by you, at as early a date as practicable, and forward it without delay, more particularly so as he is desirous that your acts should appear in their true light before the world. In it he wishes you to incorporate particularly the treatment which the prisoners belonging to your company received from the Federal authorities; also the orders issued by General Blunt or other Federal officers regarding the disposition to be made of you or your men if taken or vanquished. He has been informed that orders of a most inhuman character were issued. Indeed, he has some emanating from those holding subordinate commands, but wants to have all the facts clearly portrayed, so that the Confederacy and the world may learn the murderous and uncivilized warfare which they themselves inaugurated, and thus be able to appreciate their cowardly shrieks and howls when a just retaliation the same "measure is meted out to them." He desires me to convey to you, and through you to your command, his high appreciation of the hardships you have so nobly endured and the gallant struggle you have made against the despotism and the oppression of our State, with the confident hope that success will soon crown our efforts. I have the honor to remain, respectfully, your obedient servant, MacLean, Major and Assistant Adjutant-General.[4]

Quantrill did not reply to MacLean's letter, and his report to Price was to be his first and last to any authority. Price's assignment of the task of replying to Quantrill's report to MacLean may have been standard operating procedure, or it could have been one more indication that the troubled leader was avoiding the concept of guerrilla warfare, which went so strongly against his training and upbringing. In any case, it was obvious the beleaguered Price was looking for help from any quarter, as evidenced by his letter to Thomas C. Reynolds, the Confederate governor of Missouri, in exile at Marshall, Texas:

Camp Bragg, Ark., November 2, 1863
His Excellency Governor Thomas C. Reynolds
Marshall, Tex.:

Dear Sir: I have the honor to enclose to you an official copy of Colonel Quantrill's report of his march from Missouri River to Canadian, detailing in a terse but graphic style his attack upon Fort Baxter and upon Major-General Blunt and escort. This report was handed to me by Captain Brinker, whom you see bore a conspicuous part in the attack. Colonel Quantrill has now with him some 350 men of that daring and dashing character which has made the name of Quantrill so feared by our enemies, and have aided so much to keep Missouri, though overrun by Federals, identified with the Confederacy. The services of these men cannot be spared, but an obstacle presents itself which I fear will require more than my exertions to overcome. To engage your valuable assistance in the task is the object of this communication. It is with much regret that I find a disposition in these men to avoid coming into the service of the Confederacy. Indeed, it is this reluctance which has caused them to avoid the proximity of this army in the march southward in search of that rest which they and their horses require so much. Yet they have sent Captain Brinker to me to make known their wants as the selection of service, for as to clothing, arms, ammunition, horses. They want nothing, and indeed they are totally indifferent as to pay. They desire to serve with me as partisans, and in this they are adept, and could be made very valuable as such to the army; but for reasons which they hold good they will not come under the direct command of General Holmes, nor will they be attached to any brigade, but are willing and anxious to serve if allowed to do so as above. I have urged upon them to join regularly our army and subject themselves to such orders as its welfare might require. As it is possible they will visit your neighborhood, you could use you influence to good advantage by urging them to attach themselves to the army. Their objections are not without foundation. In the first place many of those restless spirits, chaffing under the inactivity of the army in Arkansas during the last winter and spring, deserted from General Hindman's and General Holmes' commands to seek more active scenes of operations—errors might be overlooked by an extension of the President's clemency toward deserters. Again, they have been outlawed by the Federal authorities, and expect normalcy or clemency at their hands, not even the chances of prisoners of war; and they think that if used only as scouts and rangers to ascertain and watch the movements of an enemy, they would be able to protect themselves against any surrender of our forces, should such a calamity overtake us. Captain Brinker reports to me that he has now a battalion of these men which he would bring into the service for such a purpose if allowed to place them under my immediate command. News from this quarter would be stale with you. I am glad to say that the health of the army is very much improved, and it is generally in fine condition. The Missourians, in whom you are most interested, were lately very highly complimented by Lieutenant-General Holmes for their appearance and evolutions on review.

With consideration of personal regard and esteem, I remain your obedient servant, Sterling Price[5]

Price always looked for the best in the guerrillas, or perhaps he just didn't look for the worst. In any event, he never seemed to question why they took no prisoners.

After staying at Cooper's camp for a few days, Quantrill led his weary and odorous brigade to the Red River and crossed over, without incident, into Texas.

From the Red River, the guerrillas rode to Mineral Creek, about twelve miles northeast of Sherman, and began to build shelters, little more than shacks, out of logs.

Food was no problem, for the land abounded in game and venison was a diet staple. Besides, every merchant in northeast Texas was soon to feel the impact of the dietary needs of the bushwhackers as they began looting at will.

In *The History of Grayson County* by Lucas and Hart, published in 1936, the authors state that cattle rustling ceased when Quantrill and his men came to north Texas. The bands of deserters and nonreporting conscripts who were hidden out in Jernigan Thicket and Wildcat Thicket had, indeed, been stripping farms of livestock, but why that would stop with the coming of the guerrillas is not known. It is implied that Quantrill had something to do with the rise in morality in the area, or the lack of crime, but there is no solid evidence to support such a theory.

Of course, *The History of Grayson County* also states that Quantrill came from a fine Missouri family and that Bush Smith, soon to be Bill Anderson's bride, was one of the popular young ladies of Sherman. Quantrill, of course, came from Ohio, and according to most historians, Bush Smith was a popular young lady at Chiles' saloon, as long as you had the money to pay for her favors. But Lucas and Hart, although certainly wrong about Quantrill, may have been correct about Bush Smith.

Some of the mythology surrounding Quantrill was created by writers who apparently did very little research and listened to old wives' tales.

In *Legends of the Red River,* written by Bright Ray, Quantrill is glamorized and compared to Robin Hood: "During the war years of the Sixties he [Quantrill] directed a well-disciplined company of sixty to one hundred men and from all that can be ascertained from both legend and fact not one of the band was ever known to disobey his orders or to protest his methods of organization. That in itself denotes an unusual personality. The man led a sort of Robin Hood existence; northeast Texas, from Cooke County to Lamar and sometimes as far as Jefferson on the Cypress, was his Sherwood Forest."

Ray had obviously been reading pulp fiction or the writings of John Edwards, who glamorized the role and personalities of the guerrillas.

Like Lucas and Hart, Ray also assumed that Quantrill was from a fine family in Missouri and stated, "his Robin Hood role lay in the fact that back in Clay County, Missouri, his family had been the victims of Kansas Jay-hawkers and William Charles swore vengeance against all Union soldiers and resolved to show no quarter to any of them."

But Ray could hardly be blamed for that mistake, for even his closest companions, including William Gregg, did not know until after the war that Quantrill had invented his "suffering family" excuse for being a raider. Gregg was visited by Quantrill's mother, and when he mentioned the slain older brother story, he learned that William Clarke was her oldest son.

The Reverend John H. McLean, a Methodist preacher who was in Sherman at the time, wrote fifty years after the fact:

> The day I was leaving Sherman to attend a conference in Jefferson, Quantrell [*sic*] and his men arrived in Sherman and stopped on Travis Street, in front of a little brick office I had been occupying. They were very quiet and civil in appearance. Quantrell was pointed out to me. He had a refined and civil look and was dubbed "parson" by some of his men. He was said to have been at one time a school teacher but because of certain outrages committed by Kansas Jayhawkers on the Quantrell family in Missouri, he became desperate and showed no quarter to such foes. This was told me by one who was a near neighbor of the Quantrells' in Missouri at the time the offenses were committed.[6]

The citizens of Grayson County welcomed the rebel rousers at first, but the businessmen of Sherman and the surrounding countryside would have had a good laugh, or cry, if they could have read Bright's description of Quantrill and his bandits.

The guerrillas found ways to entertain themselves, which included stealing supplies from the merchants in the county and hunting and fishing at Mineral Creek. When they got bored, they could ride into Sherman for booze and female companionship at Chiles'.

Chewing and spitting Star Navy brand chewing tobacco, whose motto was "Chew Star Navy, Spit Ham Gravy," was another way to while away the hours.

There was also horse racing, with Quantrill himself a frequent winner atop Old Charley.

Dick Mattox was the champion at breaking broncos and twirling a rope, as long as he was drunk, which was most of the time.

When all else failed, the men could always ride down the main street of Sherman, yelling and shooting at the steeple of the Methodist church.

Sherman was no sleepy hamlet, nor was it a cosmopolitan capital of the West, but with the belles of Glen Eden and the balls at Potts, the society flourished. Sherman's Dramatic Association was in full swing in 1860, as a news story reported: "This

Association is held forth nightly in a large pavilion to an interested and full audience. Saw some excellent performances. Of course, some of the company were like some in all minor theaters, not much as actors, but there were some that would have been quite respectable on a metropolitan stage. 'The Toddles,' 'The Loan of a Lover,' and 'The Hole in the Wall,' were well rendered."[7]

It is doubtful that performances were held nightly as the reporter stated, and the location of the pavilion where the plays were put on is unknown. Of course, the performances were not attended by most of the church people, as such worldly forms of entertainment were not allowed, except for Episcopalians.

The predominant church in the city was Methodist, and when Rev. John H. McLean was sent to Sherman in 1861 by the conference, succeding Rev. J. M. Brinkley, the new minister stated: "Socially and politically the communities of Marshall and Rusk and the community of Sherman were not altogether harmonious on the war question. The population of the first two communities were from the Gulf states principally, the last from such border states as Tennessee, Kentucky, Illinois, Missouri, and Kansas, and a preponderance of sentiment favored the Union."

Religious services were held regularly, and on Sunday afternoon, services were conducted for the negroes, "who were loyal to their masters and gave no trouble in the community."

The Methodist church in Sherman, like the denomination nationwide, was divided on the war issue, ultimately resulting in the division of the Church into north and south branches, but Reverend McLean managed to straddle the fence in Sherman and keep both sides content.

In 1862, a revival was held, with Maj. Joel T. Davis leading out, assisted by Reverend Hudson of the Presbyterian Church, and Mr. Flemming, who was an "exhorter" of the Confederate army.

In 1859, a new courthouse was built, but almost from the moment construction was completed, the foundation cracked and the building was so unsafe the county offices moved out of it. In 1874, T. C. Bass bought the two-story brick building for five dollars.

In 1861, A. M. Alexander's three-story brick store was the focal point of the square, and next to it was a frame structure called the Red Store, which had been moved from Preston and served as a warehouse for Alexander.

Hugh F. Young's residence was next to the Red Store, and on the corner was a blacksmith's shop.

In a small building John Dorchester practiced the trade of tinner, and it would have been natural for Quantrill, whose father was a tinner, to visit him, probably to sell him some of the little booklets his dad had written that Quantrill had sold to augment his teacher's salary before the war.

Shaw and Allen had a gunsmith's shop next to Dr. John Brooke's Drug Store, and a bakery, with its ceiling painted blue and white in a checkerboard pattern, sold pies and cakes for ten cents.

Thankfully, Ed Sacra's livery stable was set apart from the bakery. Arthur Bates and Wolf Extricher clerked in T. J. Patty's General Store, while Jim Donell managed the Sherman House.

On Jones Street, Ben Moore made sparks fly in his blacksmith's shop, and store manager John Richards sold dry goods, groceries, iron, and drugs.

On the east side of the square, G. S. Heilbroner's store had a photographer's shop, run by his son, Gabe, on the second floor, a business that was to be visited by some of Quantrill's men.

In the middle of the block was the "vilest hole in town," the Iron Post Grocery, which was really a saloon.

Other saloons included John Nelmes' "Family Grocery," which belonged to Curtis Blackwood and sold drinks for the same price as the Wagoner Bakery sold pies and cakes, ten cents.

A cobbler (who doubled as the justice of the peace) and a watchmaker were located on Houston Street, and at the corner of Houston and Travis a couple of Polish entrepreneurs dressed up their dog Chiquito to help sell their Mexican wares. They even dressed up their horse in pants in the winter.

Bird Anderson ran the hotel on the north side of the square but was to surrender its management to Ben Christian, who became a friend of Quantrill's but regretted opening his house to the guerrilla's men, at least on one occasion.

Ben Jones went off to war and left Joel Hagee as the only tailor in town, and lawyers such as Woods & Diamond, C. C. Brinkley, G. A. Edwards, and W. N. Mayrant hung out their shingles near the Anderson house.

Doctors included M. Y. Brockett, W. E. Sanders, and S. T. Hunter, and the twelve-by-fourteen-foot post office was operated by Confederate William Coffey, while Tom Bamor decorated the wagons and carriages he and his sons built with free-drawn blue roses.

While the guerrillas sat around the campfire or the hotel lobby, those of them who could read perused the *Sherman Journal.* Other papers had failed, including the *Patriot,* a black Republican paper published by a man named Foster until he was killed in 1862.

The division among Sherman residents either for or against secession was so acute that Henry Vaden reported: "Trouble began in Sherman when the Confederate flag was raised. Some men were determined it would not stay up. There was a shooting and one man was killed, another wounded. Finally Capt. Tom Bass took his shotgun and sat at the base of the flag and there was no further trouble." [8]

Sherman hardly needed any more troublemakers.

And so the stage was prepared for the events of the winter of 1863, when the Missouri guerrillas rode into town and changed the lives of the inhabitants of the sleepy little community of Sherman.

Quantrill squatted in the reddish soil of north Texas. It had been an eventful pilgrimage from the misery of Missouri, with a brief episode in Kansas at Baxter Springs, through Indian Territory, across the Red at Colbert's Ferry, and finally to his camping grounds at Mineral Creek.

There had been the exultation when they had killed the hated General Blunt at Baxter Springs, and angry, violent depression when he learned it had not been Blunt they had killed. The loss of Bledshoe only added to the agony that must have boiled within him.

But he had become used to death, and whether it was an enemy or a friend, it seemed to matter little to him unless it could be used to his advantage. He was fast becoming a very lonely man with few confidants left.

Oh, there was Todd, he perhaps hoped, who would stay devoted to the charismatic leader. But Fletcher was not to trusted, and Anderson had apparently lost his mind, or was in the process of doing so. Quantrill must have wondered if he had ever been sane.

The captured hearse had been taken from the Federals at Baxter Springs and had carried Bledshoe until he died and was buried in a shallow grave, along with the negro who dug their graves in south Indian Territory, but it was of no use to the guerrilla leader now and he had sent Fletcher into Sherman to trade it for coffee.

He may have wished that he had brought Kate to Texas with him, for the nights were cold and he missed the warmth of her teenage body, but it was best she stayed in Missouri. If it came down to it, he could get a woman at Chiles' in Sherman to satisfy his carnality.

Over at Bonham, Gen. Henry McCulloch received word of the arrival of the bushwhackers with mixed emotions, and on October 22, 1863, he wrote to Capt. Edmund P. Turner, the assistant adjutant general:

> Captain: A good many of Colonel Quantrill's command have come into this sub-district, and it is said that he is now within it. He has not reported here, and I do not know what his military status is. I do not know much about his mode of warfare as others seem to know; but, from all I can learn, is it but little, if at all, removed from that of the wildest savage; so much so, that I do not for a moment believe that our Government can sanction it in one of her officers. Hence, it seems to me if he be an officer of our army, his conduct should be officially noticed, and if he be not an officer of our army, his acts should be disavowed by our Government, and as far as practicable, he be made to understand that we would greatly prefer his remaining away from our army or its vicinity.
>
> I appreciate his services, and am anxious to have them; but certainly we cannot, as a Christian people, sanction a savage inhuman warfare, in which men are to be shot down like dogs, after throwing down their arms and holding up their hands supplicating for mercy.
>
> This is a matter to which I wish to call the serious attention of our commanding generals, and with regard to which I desire their advice and instructions as early as practicable.
> Henry E. McCulloch
> Brigadier-General, Commanding Northern Sub-District[9]

Unfortunately for McCulloch, his commanding officer, Gen. Edmund Kirby Smith, did not share his disdain for the guerrillas and was determined to find a practical use for their unmilitary mode of operation. Smith, a devout Christian, was prone to let his religion get in the way of his military objectives at times, but perhaps, like Sterling Price, he was desperate to find someone who would fight Yankees, regardless of their techniques.

Smith saw a use for Quantrill in northeast Texas in rounding up the deserters from the Confederate army who had taken to the brush to keep from fighting anymore. Along with conscripts who had failed to report for military duty, they had formed bands in the Texas countryside, hiding out in brush, woods, and swamps much like Quantrill and his men had done in Missouri.[10]

What better way to catch a bushwhacker than to send a bushwhacker in after them? And so Smith dispatched a letter to McCulloch:

> If you resort to force in bringing back the absentees and collecting the conscripts in your district, no better force could be employed than that of Quantrill's Missourians. Their not being from the state, will make them more effective. They are bold, fearless men, and, moreover, from all representations, are under very fair discipline. They are composed, I understand, in a measure of the very best class of Missourians. They have suffered every outrage in their person and families at the hands of the Federals, and being outlawed and their lives forfeited, have waged a war of no quarter whenever they have come in contact with the enemy.

The purpose of the mission was to bring the deserters and conscripts in so they could help fill the empty ranks of the Confederate army, but Quantrill and his raiders made a raid on Jernigan (or Wildcat) Thicket and killed more deserters than they brought back, proving McCulloch's theory that the bandits were useless for regular military service. Besides, Quantrill and his men disliked the job, perhaps because there was not much booty to be taken from a dead deserter. Probably they were sympathetic to men who refused to fight a war among the ranks of a regular army.

Quantrill and his men agreed to the assignment of routing out the men in the brush because of the promise of ammunition, guns, and rations, but the trusting Kirby Smith was soon to learn that "the very best class of Missourians" were not to be trusted.

On November 19, 1863, Aide-de-Camp Lt. E. Cunningham wrote yet another communication to General McCulloch, who seemed to be caught in the middle:

> General; The Lieutenant General commanding directs me to say that Captain Quantrill leaves Shreveport to-day to join his command, and passes your headquarters en route.
>
> He is informed by this officer that several of his men, who he regards as entirely reliable, went to the rendezvous of the deserters in your district, pretending that they also had deserted from their commands. They mixed among those outlaws freely, and they, thinking that Captain Quanrtill himself was not loyal to our Government, fully disclosed their conditions and plans. Captain Quantrill thinks that in giving themselves up to you it has been simply their purpose to get arms and ammunition, of which they were in need, so that in the spring they can go north. This they are resolved to do. It is the opinion of the commanding General that these men are unreliable, and should be trusted in nothing. He disapproves of your agreement with them, and thereby relieves you from all responsibility as to its fulfillment . . .

But McCulloch's headaches with the guerrillas were only beginning, and by February of 1864, he was probably praying for an early spring so the troublemaking marauders would pack their ponies and head north. To Maj. Gen. J. B. Magruder, who was commanding the District of Texas, he wrote on February 15:

> Quantrill will not obey orders, and so much mischief is charged to his command here that I have determined to disarm, arrest, and send his entire command to you or General Smith. This is the only chance to get them out of this section of country, which they have nearly ruined, and I have never yet got them to do any service. Whenever orders have gone to them they have some excuse, but are certain not to go. In one instance the enrolling officer of Grayson County sent them to impress some whisky at a distillery, under my orders, based upon yours, and they got into a row, killed one man, and

plundered the still house and dwelling, and the next night went back and burned the still-house, but nothing can be proven on them, because the people are afraid to swear against them. They regard the life of a man less than you would that of a sheep-killing dog. My plan now is to arrest Quantrill's men, send you about 100 returned deserters for you to dispose of, and then arrest the rest of the brush crowd, send them to Shreveport, and do all I can to arrest all deserters, those who harbor them, and those who openly avow disloyal sentiments.[11]

It was a threat the beleaguered general would never be able to accomplish, of course, for the guerrillas under Quantrill and the brush men hiding out from Confederate service could avoid troops easily in the thickness of Jernigan Thicket and the woods of Grayson County.

Next the guerrillas were given an opportunity to fight Indians. When a raiding party of Comanches attacked Gainesville, McCulloch sent Quantrill and his men after them. They soon learned, however, that despite their astute horsemanship and ability to operate in the brush, they were no match for the Comanches in their own territory. The guerrillas could never catch them.

They also chased a threatening small force of Federals north into Oklahoma in December. It was the revenge attack for the massacre at Baxter Springs.

And over at Bonham, weeping Henry did what he did best, sent out a dispatch complaining of his resources.

Headquarters Northern Sub-District of Texas
Bonham, December 22, 1863
Capt. Edmund P. Turner
Assistant Adjutant-General, Houston;
Captain: News of a reliable character reached me this morning at daybreak that the Indians or jayhawkers in considerable force (number not known) had penetrated as far as Gainesville at 9 o'clock last night and news of a less reliable character has just come in that they occupied that place this morning, Indians and Federals, 400 strong.
I sent all the cavalry force I had this morning at 8 o'clock, numbering only some 200 men, from this place, directing

Quantrill, from Sherman, to meet them at once, and have sent orders to all of Colonel Martin's companies that are within reach to concentrate at McKinney and Pilot Grove, to move forward as rapidly as possible.

If the last report be true, it is the advance of a Federal and Jayhawker force, or a heavy raid of same character.

I have not more than 150 infantry here, and all the cavalry I can concentrate in three days will not amount to over 500, and not s single piece of artillery, from which you will see but too plainly that I have no force to defend the granary of Texas with if I should be called upon to do so. A general without troops is worth but little in defending his country.

Most Respectfully, &c., Henry E. McCulloch

Brigadier-General, Commanding Northern Sub-District[12]

For once, the guerrillas, with a little help from their friends, accomplished their assignment, for they caught the force, made up of Kansas Jayhawkers and Union Cavalry. Confederate Choctaw Indians reported that only a handful of the troops escaped. Quantrill's men celebrated by going to Sherman and getting drunk.

General McCulloch was obviously an educated and brilliant man, but sending Quantrill's men to break up the moonshine stills in north Texas was not the smartest thing he ever did. The guerrillas were the best customers of the stills, and although they did break up one operation, kill one man, and burn the still, they kept the whiskey for personal use, while most of the moonshiners continued to operate and supply their best customers, the bushwhackers.

It was obvious to Henry that the bushwhackers had little or no interest in furthering the Southern cause, especially in northeast Texas. Or probably anyplace else.

CHAPTER 6

Sophia

Sophia Butt's spirit probably wandered back to the old days, when parties at Glen Eden were more elegant, at least as far as the guest list was concerned. Now there were only a few very young men and many old men from Grayson County left to attend her parties, for most of the manhood of the area had gone off to war or were hiding in Jernigan or Wildcat thickets to avoid conscription. There were more Yankees in northeast Texas than Confederates, if you were to judge by the secession vote, and thousands of these were among the brush men, along with a goodly number of Confederate deserters, and according to some reports, even some Northern Yankee deserters.

But of course, there was the presence of Quantrill's Missourians, who were certain to add to the excitement of the occasion.

In the early days the parties were attended by many of the elite, including officers from nearby Fort Washita such as Albert Sidney Johnston and the young lieutenants Sam Grant and Bob Lee. Other guests had included John Hood and J.E.B. Stuart as they made there way to the frontier or the Mexican war.

Sophia must have recalled the prim and proper Lee, as opposed to the poorly postured Grant in his rumpled clothes. One of her prized possessions was a rocking chair that was given to Colonel Coffee in 1842 by Gen. W. L. Marcy and had been occupied by Lee.

While president, Grant wrote Sophia, inviting her to visit the

White House. At Appomatox, Grant reminded Lee that they had met once in Mexico, but Lee didn't remember, so they probably never were at Sophia's at the same time.

Johnston commanded Fort Washita, which was only about twenty-five miles from Glen Eden. Destiny had great plans for the young officers who would later face each other in combat.

After Sophia's first husband, Jesse Augustine Aughinbaugh, had brought her from Indiana to Texas in 1838, he left her at old Washington and disappeared, abandoning his young teenage bride without money or skills to make a living, except perhaps one. There were rumors about why he left, but nothing had been proven.

Sophia had come from a military family, her father, William Suttenfield, served in the army until 1816 and then opened a trading post for Indians and operated as a supplier at Fort Wayne, Indiana.

To add to her both military and social upbringing, Sophia grew to be a beautiful young lady and broke her father's heart when she ran off to Texas with the German officer.

After Aughinbaugh dumped her, she supposedly practiced the oldest profession in the world, which may very well have been the reason he left her. But the question as to whether she was a professional or an amateur has never been proven.

Like most of the players on the stage of Grayson County in 1863, Sophia was an enigma. Sherrie McLeRoy, Grayson County historian and author of *Mistress of Glen Eden,* says in her preface to that booklet: "And her contemporaries were sharply divided in their opinion of her; was she just a beautiful woman with too much natural charm for her own good? Or was she a Jezebel who used men to achieve her own ends? I've spent four years now researching the life and times of Sophia Suttonfield Aughinbaugh Coffee Butt Porter, and I still can't answer those questions. There are so many stories about Sophie, some of which she originated herself, that sorting the truth from the fiction is a nearly impossible task."[1]

Sophia had the gift of beauty and the ability to make a man feel important, twin talents that could produce at least a livelihood and catch the eye of even such an important figure as Sam Houston.

Some had called her a friend, even a protegée, of Houston's, but rumors said she was much more, and when she nursed him back to health after he was wounded at the Battle of San Jacinto, (at least that was Sophia's story), their relationship became a long-term devotion to each other.

She considered it providential that she had been present as one of the refugees at San Jacinto, although some have used the term "camp follower."

When Sophia later married Holland Coffee, Sam had been a guest in their home, but the past was probably never discussed. What transpired between them was their own well-kept secret. The fact that Sophia is not mentioned in Houston's memoirs is not surprising. Colonel Coffee would not understand anything but a platonic relationship between the two, and besides, when he wrote his memoirs, Sam had espoused the Baptist religion. Perhaps when he was baptized in Nacogdoches, in additon to having his sins forgiven, his memory was washed clean.

When Grayson County was established out of Fannin County, Houston had been the speaker at the ceremonies in Sherman and stayed with Sophia at Glen Eden. On the hot summer day he spoke, she held an umbrella to protect him from the sun.

Some speculated, when Colonel Coffee brought Sophia to Grayson County, that perhaps wedding vows had not been ex-changed, but the first ball held in the county was at the fort in honor of the bride and groom.

Sophia met Colonel Coffee either in Waco or in a stockade where they had both sought protection from the war, and they were married in 1838, with Houston present to dance with the bride.

She moved to Grayson County (then part of Fannin County) with her new husband. The horseback trip covered some five hundred miles and required a military escort from Fort Warren through the dangerous woods filled with Indians.

Sophia gave a vivid description of her first home with Holland: "We lived in a clap-board house with puncheon floors, and our table consisted of a good's box with legs on it. The first quilt I had in Grayson County, I picked the cotton out with my fingers, and Col. Coffee laid the quilt off with a square, and I quilted it. I then made me a rag carpet and put it on the puncheon floor, and a goods box nailed up on the side of the wall was my wardrobe. And on viewing the carpet, quilt, and wardrobe I was the happiest woman in Texas."

In 1843 Coffee and Sophia built a two-story southern-style mansion called Glen Eden, and Houston was said to have been a frequent visitor, along with a parade of United States officers on their way to and from the Mexican War. Visitors included Capt. Albert Sidney Johnson and young lieutenants Robert E. Lee and Ulysses S. Grant.

Glen Eden soon became the social center of northeast Texas, and parties hosted by Sophia sometimes lasted for days and nights, while the young people danced to the music of flute, violin, and banjo. The parties became so popular that sometimes the young people of Sherman would show up sans invitation, and even these impromptu events still sometimes lasted for days.

When Coffee was killed in a saloon in 1846, he left the widow not only Glen Eden, but enough funds to continue her lifestyle. His death cast a shadow on her reputation, however. Charles Galloway had supposedly been spreading rumors about liaisons Sophia had been having with several men, including Justice of the Peace Thomas Murphy, and when she had strongly urged Holland to give Galloway a good horsewhipping, he refused. Sophia told him she would rather be married to a dead hero than a live coward.

Apparently, Holland had seen it coming, for he had added a codicil to his will to correct the fact that he had failed to word his will correctly so Sophia would not have to post a bond. The codicil began: "And I, Holland Coffee, being apprehensive that surrounding circumstances may soon terminate my life..." In the summer of 1846, Galloway killed Holland at the combination grocery and saloon at Preston Bend.

On a trip to New Orleans in 1852, Sophia met Maj. George Butt, from Norfolk, Virginia, who was there to sell the remains of his plantation. Their marriage was the social event of the era.

The wedding was remembered by Helen Cummins of Sherman as an event that brought young people from all over northeast Texas to Glen Eden for the ceremony and celebration that followed. Mrs. Cummins remembered that her father, Dr.

Morrison, unable to obtain white kid gloves, wore a pair made from the skin of a white dog.

The wedding lasted until Butt was murdered by one of Quantrill's men.

Quantrill had not only visited but had been a house guest at Glen Eden during his short stay in Texas in the winter of 1862. A quiet, polite man, he had been a delight to Sophia and her other guests.

Obviously educated, he knew the little secrets of society that brought acceptance. It was only when she looked into his strangely hued violet eyes that she must have felt a fear she could not explain.

But Bill would be a welcome guest at her party, along with a few of his officers, if indeed, they were really officers in the Confederate army. Having entertained generals and generals-to-be, Sophia knew an officer when she met one, and Quantrill was the only one of the guerrilla band who came even close to fitting the image.

Sophia had thrown so many parties that it had become second nature to her, and although there were many things to check on, from the oven filled with fresh baking bread to the egg nog, she took it all in stride. Even when emergencies occurred, she responded by assigning one of the slaves to the problem. The parties past had been extravagant and orchestrated.

But wartime dictated a containment of luxury, due to an extreme shortage of the supplies that added refinement to frontier living, and also owing to the fact that so many of the men of Grayson County were in the Confederate army. For the most part, only very young and very old men remained for the girls to flirt with.

But the presence of Quantrill and his Missourians in the area must have added a new anticipation to a party.

The young ladies of Sherman, at least at first, seemed to be enchanted by the lack of refinement in the guerrillas, and their reputation for killing and raucous living only added to the intrigue. The local men must have looked with envy on the fine horses the guerrillas rode, for most of them had lost all their good horseflesh to the Confederate cause, or to thieving Confederate deserters or Yankee sympathizers. But the welcome mat the citizens of Grayson County had put out so eagerly for the Missourians was about to wear thin.

Parties, along with the prosperity and abundance of Glen Eden, had left Sophia a little on the plump side, at least compared to the days when she tickled Sam Houston's fancy, but her charm overcame age and obesity.

Glen Eden was a marvel for the time, a magnificent oasis in the brush of north Texas. The galleries were broad and the rooms spacious. But the real beauty was in the flower gardens across the front of the home, along with the catalpa trees whose seeds had been brought to Sophia from California by none less than Albert Sidney Johnston. Her flower beds and walkways were lined with a collection of rocks, brought to her by admirers from all over the western territories.

CHAPTER 7

Quantrill and the Rebellious Rebel Wives

The little boy from Canal Dover, Ohio, who enjoyed torturing animals had come a long way. From distorted reports by his contemporaries, and exaggerated historical reviews and dime novels, he had become the epitome of Confederate patriotism to some and the devil incarnate to others. But contrary to the "Legends of the Red River," he was certainly not a modern-day Robin Hood.

Regardless of your opinion of the violet-eyed killer, there is no doubt that he was a charismatic personality who was able to bend men's minds to accomplish his will, at least for a time.

He could be a demon, or an angel of light, depending on the circumstances and what was in it for Quantrill.

One of those who fell victim to the Quantrill charm was John Potts, owner of one of the largest plantations in north Texas, located in the Preston Bend area, the man Pottsboro was named for.

Potts had moved his operations, along with his 100 slaves, to Texas from Mississippi, probably because he foresaw the impending conflict and, like many others, thought that Texas' wide expanse would be a safer place than the Deep South if a civil war began.

Like Sophia and Major Butt at nearby Glen Eden, the Potts residence was a focal point for social activity and Quantrill was a welcome guest.

Besides, Potts was losing a lot of cattle to rustlers, and it was reported that the thievery stopped when Quantrill and his men came to Texas. There are, however, no reports of the Missourians actually capturing or killing any rustlers.

A story in the *Sherman Herald-Democrat* on September 1, 1926, gives an account of a letter Quantrill wrote to Mrs. Potts from Missouri.

At that time, the writer, E. J. Parker, reported the letter was in the possession of Mrs. J. M. Steele of Woodville, Oklahoma, a cousin of county auditor Allie S. Noble of Sherman.

There are a couple of problems with this letter. First, it is dated December 12, 1863, and sent from Camp Lookout.[1] Parker also states that just before Christmas 1863, Quantrill and his men made a sudden departure from Texas.

All accounts show Quantrill and his men in Grayson County in 1863 and into the spring of 1864. One possible explanation is that the event took place in the winter of 1862, for it is known that Quantrill was in Texas then for a short period of time. But it interesting to note that Quantrill presented Mrs. Potts with a gift of coffee, hard to get in the South, and he had sold the hearse he had taken at Fort Blair and bought a quantity of coffee in the fall of 1863.

> Mrs. Potts—
> After my compliments, you will allow me to present you with some coffee. And, in consideration of your kindness to my men who have been at your house, we are all under obligations to you and your daughters and when we are far off in danger we will often think of the hospitality received at your hands. And should it happen that the enemy should invade your home, you will remember that we will strike a blow for you all. My respects to all your family.
> Respectively yours, W. C. Quantrell.

The story also reports that in 1864 Quantrill and his raiders repelled a Yankee attack on the Potts Plantation. Parker states later in the story that "when Quantrell [*sic*], the James boys and others returned to Sherman in 1864, they struck camp in Northeast Sherman, on the spot where the W. H. Lucas store is located on North Broughton Street."

It seems obvious that Parker, or his source, had gotten their dates mixed up.

Dick Hopson, who was in Grayson County during the war, knew Quantrill personally and in 1926 gave his account of the time Sherman was besieged by a mob of angry Confederate wives and widows and was emancipated by that benefactor of all mankind, William Clarke Quantrill.

The Southern Confederacy, for the last two years of its existence, maintained in the county site of all organized counties a commissary department, where was kept all kinds of foodstuffs which that particular county produced. This produce was raised by a sort of tithing process. From these commissaries rations could be drawn by passing soldiers, and all 'war widows' were privileged to draw rations also. The number of 'war widows' was very large in Grayson County, and may of them needed these war rations very much. Texas had sent between 50,000 and 60,000 of its men to the war.

The officer in charge of the Sherman commissary was Major Blaine, a veteran of the Texas War for Independence and the father of John M. Blaine, for many years chief of police of Sherman. By reason of bountiful crops, the Sherman commissary was unusually well supplied with grain, flour, and meal, and became well known to all the war widows in the county. However, they became dissatisfied with the sameness of the rations they were permitted to draw. By this time, the trade between Texas and Mexico had developed into greater proportions. Cotton raised in Texas was hauled to the Rio Grande, sold for a big price, and the money invested in such necessary supplies as the blockade had deprived, and you could buy most anything in the principal towns if you had gold coin with which to pay for it.

Now, some propagandist started the rumor among the war widows of Grayson County that this trade was all being carried on by the government, and that all of those commodities, including the luxuries, among which were coffee and tea, had been purchased by the government for the use of the families of the soldiers, but that the officers in charge were selling them to the people or shipping them to Mexico and keeping the money. This report resulted in a secret organization of war widows, determined to have what was coming to them. This organization was especially strong in north Texas counties, and also in East Texas.

One day in the winter of 1864, the city of Sherman found itself in the hands of a mob of wild-eyed, desperate women, armed with guns, axes, sledge hammers, and clubs. The mob numbered more than 125, and the members came on horse-back. The leader was a Mrs. Savage. She was a born leader, and had she been a man would at least have been a general in the army of the Confederacy. Those who came with her obeyed her every command. The mob surrounded the commissary and Mrs. Savage, being the spokesman told Major Blaine that she knew soldier's rations contained coffee and tea, and that he had been withholding these things from rations of the 'war widows' of Grayson County. She added that they had come for what belonged to them and would stand no foolishness.

Major Blaine very gracefully surrendered. Producing the keys, he escorted the ladies through his warehouse, showing them that he had none of those things. The ladies were not satisfied and argued that what they sought was in some other building. Most of the business houses were locked up and empty. To these the women now turned their attention and with hammers and axes continued their quest, searching in vain for the much coveted luxuries.

On the east side of the square was a general store kept by I. H. Hellbroner, a subject of Great Britain. He had quite a good stock of goods brought to Sherman from Mexico. At the first sign of trouble he locked his doors and got out of the way. In due course the mob—and it was a wild mob now, a number of Sherman women having joined it—reached the store, broke down the doors and were helping themselves when the unexpected happened.[2]

At this point, Quantrill just happened to ride up, and Hopson said his very appearance made the women stop their raiding of the store.

In a quiet voice, he shamed the women, reminding them that their husbands were at the front enduring terrible hardships. He talked of their lack of food and shoes and how they were doing their duty without complaining.

It took a while, but the women finally calmed down and abandoned their quest for coffee and tea and even nailed the doors to the store back up as they left.

In a story in the *Sherman Herald-Democrat* in September of

1926, reporter E. J. Parker related the story of the Potts letter and Quantrill's taming of the angry Confederate women, but there are errors in his story.

He states that Quantrill and his men came to Sherman in the spring of 1863 and left in December of that year, but the story of the angry wives is true and pretty much as he relates it.

The story would seem almost invented if you did not know the character of Quantrill and his ability to control minds. He could appear to be an angel of light, or the devil from the depths of hell, depending on the personalities involved and what was to be gained, either in the way of loot or to enhance his reputation.

CHAPTER 8

The Beginning of the End

Quantrill sensed that the whole thing was beginning to fall apart. Using the horror of the prison collapse in Kansas City, he had been in complete control of his troops through the Lawrence raid, although for the sake of posterity, he was to claim that the men had gotten out of control and acted on their own after getting drunk.

But since then, he had heard the whispered dissension begin to grow among the men. Some were upset because the loot had not been properly divided among them, and others had been repulsed by the killing of innocents.

Probably those who had families on the western border of Missouri could see little difference between the atrocities committed by the Federals under Ewing's Order No. 11 and their own destruction of the homes of the Lawrence residents. Only a few of them knew that Quantrill's slaughter of the innocents had been for personal revenge.

Before the trek to Texas, the raiders, led by Gregg, had made "attacks" on Missouri City and Plattsburg. Fletch Taylor and James Little were volunteers on these raids, although they were normally Todd's men.

When Taylor and Little stole six thousand dollars and refused to split it with Gregg, hard feelings began to brew. At the home of Mrs. David George, Gregg confronted Todd and

Quantrill with the matter and, of course, Todd backed his men, while Quantrill sided with him. The first crack in the foundation of the organization had appeared.

A division with Bill Anderson, which began perhaps at Baxter Springs when Quantrill refused to continue the attack on Fort Blair, was renewed when one of Anderson's men stole a bolt of cloth and Quantrill made him return it. He exiled the man, named Madison, to the north side of the Red River, but when Madison returned and murdered a citizen, Quantrill had him killed. Anderson, of course, was furious.

And so when William Gregg came to him in Sherman to tell him he was leaving, Quantrill could see the crack becoming a chasm and the erosion of his command beginning to materialize.

"You have been a good soldier and a good officer, and an honest man, " he said to Gregg. "I have no fault to find with you, but I think it best that you should go away. You have enemies in camp."

"Who are these enemies?" asked Gregg.

"Why, there are Taylor and Little, whom you denounced as thieves, and Barker don't like you first rate," said Quantrill.

"Well," said Gregg, "are not these men thieves?"

"Yes," said Quantrill, "they are."

"Now," replied Gregg, "you say that I have been a good soldier and officer and an honest man. Why do you want me to leave and the thieves to stay?"

Quantrill mumbled something about Gregg being a captain and his influence on the men.

"Well," said Gregg, "I came to tell you I was leaving to join the regular Confederate forces and I would like for you to give me a leave of absence so I can go report to General McCulloch."[1]

Quantrill wrote the pass for ninety days and watched as Gregg rode off toward Sherman. It was, he thought, one of the first of his officers to desert him, and he must have known it would not be the last. In all probability, Cole Younger had already deserted for California by this time.

Historians would differ on whether Gregg left of his own accord or was asked to leave by Quantrill for his own safety, but the results were the same—it was all beginning to slip away.

Gregg managed to avoid his enemies on the trail by stopping at an inn on the way to Sherman but probably would have been killed there had it not been for Fletcher Taylor, who told George Todd, "I will not kill Gregg. He is a Southern man, and he has been a good soldier and officer. If you want him killed you will have to kill him yourself." [2]

Inside the mind of the demonical killer Todd, the urge to murder Gregg was quieted by his fear of his potential victim, Fletcher Taylor, or Quantrill, to whom he was still, at least on the surface, loyal.

Henry McCulloch was not the type of man who sought recognition, but he was beginning to realize that history would remember him as the little brother of Ben McCulloch, who fought at San Jacinto and had been a leader of the Texas Rangers. His death at the Battle of Pea Ridge only enhanced the mystique of his dynamic personality.

Unlike his older brother, Henry had spent the war confined inside the borders of Texas, except for one sojourn with Maj. Gen. John G. Walker's division in a failed effort to relieve the siege of Vicksburg.

In a letter to W. W. Scott, postmarked Harrison, Arkansas, February 19, 1896, W. L. Potter expressed his opinion of McCulloch by calling him "the Feather Bed General of the Northern Sub District of Texas," and added: "Gen McCullough [*sic*] feasted on confederate Rations Until the collapse of the so called confederate States of America in April 1865.

"When McCullough & his staff with several Ambulances well filled with the Most Valuable confederate supplies, took the road through Dallas to his home in southern or in central Texas. What became of him after that I never heard." [3]

Most of his war was spent posting Confederate garrisons along the eastern edge of the Texas Panhandle, dealing with Indian raids, the thousands of deserters who filled the brush country of northeast Texas, and the infiltration into the area by the undisciplined and drunken bushwhackers from Missouri.

His plan to rid the district of moonshiners by sending Quantrill's raiders out to destroy the stills had been a disaster, since all the Missourians did was wreck a few of the burst-head operations in favor of those they did business with, and carried the confiscated whiskey back to their camp at Mineral Creek.

He had also sent them to chase Indians who had made a raid

on Gainesville, but even the superior horses of the bushwhackers could not catch the resourceful Comanches who knew the territory and either outran or outwitted their drunk pursuers.

Finally, pressed by Gen. Kirby Smith, commander of the Trans-Mississippi Department, to find a use for the ornery visitors from the north, he sent them out to Jernigan swamp to round up deserters from the Confederate army and a multitude of young men who seemed committed to fighting for neither side.

But capturing prisoners was not Quantrill's style, and he and his men killed about as many of the renegades as they returned for Confederate service.

McCulloch had finally decided that his first impression had been correct and the psuedo-Confederates from Missouri were nothing but criminals and of no use whatsoever to the Southern cause. He decided that Smith, who sometimes let his Christianity get in the way of his judgment, knew nothing of the character of the bushwhackers and that Sterling Price knew exactly what they were, but in desperation, he was ready to praise a rattlesnake if it would bite a Yankee.

And now McCulloch sat in his office at Bonham, brooding over the latest reports from Grayson County and wondering if he should have accepted the nomination for governor instead of remaining in the military. But it was too late, and he knew he must find a way to deal with the rowdy gang who claimed to be Confederate soldiers and whose leader claimed to be a colonel in the army of the South.

He could hope for an opportunity to expel the raiders from his district, or he could look for an excuse to destroy them completely, an option he did not relish, for the regular soldiers he had sent out seemed prone not to engage the Missourians in combat. Their sluggish weapons and tactics were no match for the firepower of a bushwhacker with a pistol in each hand, firing in two directions while riding at full speed on a fine horse.

Finally he decided his best course of action was to pray for an early spring. But he was soon to learn that fate had cast him in an important role in the break-up of the guerrillas.

CHAPTER 9

Party Time!

Their service as a military unit was not appreciated by the Confederate authorities, so the raiders from the north spent their days in Sherman racing horses and stealing what they could from the local merchants, and spent their nights getting drunk, either at Chiles' gambling den and part-time house of ill repute, at the Iron Post Grocery, or at the camp at Mineral Creek.

Quantrill was the most frequent winner of the races on his horse Old Charley.

Dick Maddox was drunk again. Or he was still drunk. It was hard to tell if Dick ever sobered up, except that when he was drunk, he was the best rider around and when he was sober, he could hardly stay on a horse.

When he was drunk he was also a trickster with a rope, and since he was drunk most of the time, he could be a very entertaining fellow.

And while Dick twirled his rope, some of the other members of Quantrill's gang shot holes in the globe on top of the Methodist church. Sherman had become a very lively place, and it was only midafternoon and wasn't even Saturday.

It was Thursday, December 24, 1863, Christmas Eve, and for the decent folks of Sherman, the hope of having a quiet celebration of the holiday was fading fast.

Inside Ben Christian's hotel on the north side of the square, guests were preparing for a somber observance of the holy day by having a dance, while on the east side of the dumpy two-story courthouse with the squatty roof, a celebration of another sort was just getting underway at the Iron Post Grocery, which in reality was a saloon, and the vilest one in Sherman.

The Heilbroner store was about the only business open on that side of the square, except for Gabe Heilbroner's photo gallery on the second floor.

William Coffey, the postmaster, was trying to figure out how to replace the lock that had been shot off of the door of the twelve-by-fourteen-foot post office by one of the celebrants.

The west side of the square was dominated by the three-story brick store which was built by A. M. Alexander.

The excitement of the arrival and departure of the Butterfield stage was gone with the war. The operation was too easy a target for outlaws.

Inside the Ben Christian Hotel, Sophia Butt waited for the festivities to begin, little dreaming that she would play a major role in the raiders' Christmas cheer.

Sophia must have wondered as she heard the celebrants outside the hotel if it would not be unwise for a lady to go out into the streets of Sherman that night.

As the darkness of winter night swept over the city, the noise outside increased. The voices from down at the saloon became louder, and there was an occasional sound of the breaking of glass, punctuated with pistol shots, probably aimed at the globe atop the Methodist church.

But it was at Chiles' house where some of the revelers began drinking all the egg nog, then found a barrel of whiskey and finished it off.

Next they rode into the square, hollering and shooting their pistols in the air.

One rode his horse up on the porch of the hotel, its hooves breaking through the boards. Encouraged by his companions, he rode the animal right into the lobby of the hotel!

Sophia and the other guests stood in shock as the drunken marauders entered the room. The rider pointed the gun directly at Sophia and it exploded. She must have felt the nearness of the bullet as it took one of the tassels off the top of her hat.

It didn't take long for the drunken gang to decide they

wanted to have their picture made and they headed for Heilbroner's studio. Either they were unhappy with the images or were just in a hell-raising mood, because they destroyed Gabe's studio and equipment.

The next day, hung over, they sheepishly returned to Sherman (under orders from Quantrill) to apologize and pay for the damage they had done.

Probably the lack of respect shown to Sophia was what outraged the guerrilla leader the most, for she was a lady who had welcomed and befriended the usurpers from Missouri and they had repaid her hospitality by shooting at her hat and would soon make her husband a target.

The next fling of the guerrillas was a New Year's dance at Jim Crow Chiles'. The problem with this party was that not all of the men got an invite and so some decided to crash the party. The fight between the crashers and the invitees resulted in only bruised fists and feelings, but once again, Quantrill was called in to subdue the savage beasts.

Meanwhile, over in Bonham, Henry McCulloch had just about thrown up his hands and probably wished he could head for Gaudalupe County and his farm. He had received a letter from Kirby Smith dated November 2, 1863, with instructions on what to do with Quantrill and his men:

> If you resort to force in bringing back the absentees and collecting the conscripts in your district, no better force could be employed than that of Quantrill's Missourians. Their not being from the State, will make them more effective. They are bold, fearless men, and, moreover from all representations, are under very fair discipline. They are composed, I understand, in a measure of the very best class of Missourians. They have suffered every outrage in their person and families at the hands of the Federals,and, being outlawed and their lives forfeited, have waged a war of no quarter, whenever they have come in contact with the enemy. Colonel Quantrill, I understand, will perform the duty, provided rations and forage are issued to his men and horses; this you are authorized to order. In the event you have no immediate service for him and his command, direct him to report in person at these headquarters. His command should go into camp at some convenient

point; where they could receive rations and forage until Colonel Quantrill's return.

Since writing the above, a second letter from you of 23rd October has been received. You can issue the rations and forage required for Quantrill's command, provided they remain under your command. The best disposition you can make of them will be in breaking up and bringing in the bands of deserters in your district.

I am, general, very respectfully, your obedient servant,
E. Kirby Smith
Lieutenant-General[1]

The general seemed to be convinced that Quantrill was a Confederate soldier and patriot, since he described him as "Colonel" Quantrill. And again, the leadership of the Confederacy seemed to be convinced that Quantrill was from a fine Missouri family and loyal to the cause of the South.

McCulloch must have hyperventilated when he read Smith's letter. He must have also seriously considered the general's advice to send Quantrill to Shreveport, along with his own suggestion as to what Smith could do with him.

But on November 19, 1863, he received another letter, not from Smith, but from his aide-de-camp, Lt. E. Cunningham.

Apparently Quantrill had made his visit to Smith and reported on clandestine operations that he and his men had performed among the deserters. Quantrill must have turned on the charm and convinced the general that McCulloch's plan for recovering the brush men was all wrong and the guerrilla way, killing them, was the proper solution to the problem.

Perhaps that is why Smith had his aide write the letter complaining of McCulloch's "agreement" with the deserters. It is interesting to note that Quantrill got demoted from colonel to captain.

Headquarters Trans-Mississippi Department
Shreveport, La., November 19, 1863

Brig. Gen Henry E. McCulloch,
Commanding &e., Bonham, Tex.:

GENERAL: The lieutenant-general commanding directs

me to say that Captain Quantrill leaves Shreveport to-day to join his command, and passes your headquarters en route.

He is informed by this officer that several of his men, whom he regards as entirely reliable, went to the rendezvous of the deserters in your district, pretending that they also had deserted from their commands. They mixed among these outlaws freely, and they, thinking that Captain Quantrill himself was not loyal to our Government, fully disclosed their condition and plans. Captain Quantrill thinks that in giving themselves up to you it has been simply their purpose to get arms and ammunition, of which they were in need, so that in the spring they can go north. This they are resolved to do. It is the opinion of the commanding general that these men are unreliable, and should be trusted in nothing. He disapproves of your agreement with them, and thereby relieves you from all responsibility as to its fulfillment.

The concession to them of the privilege of serving where they are would increase the number of desertions, and greatly demoralize the troops in the commands from which they have deserted. He therefore directs that all those who have already given themselves up be sent to their commands immediately. The horses of such as do not belong to the cavalry will be purchased for the Government, in accordance with General Orders, No. 37 and 53, from Adjutant and Inspector General's Office, Richmond. The horses of those who hereafter give themselves up voluntarily shall be similarly disposed of.

The lieutenant general commanding thinks that the only thing to be done now is to go vigorously to work, and kill or capture all those who refuse to come in. The commanding general thinks the ringleaders should have no quarter.

I am, sir, very respectively, your obedient servant,

E. Cunningham

Lieutenant, and Aide-de-Camp[2]

It should be remembered that all the men in the brush were not deserters from the Confederate army, but many of them were citizens of north Texas, opposed to secession, who refused to be drafted into the army and took to the brush to avoid conscription.

On February 3, 1864, McCulloch wrote to Maj. Gen. J. B. Magruder, complaining about how large his district was and his lack of troops needed to carry out General Smith's order to round up the deserters hidden in the brush and send them back to their commands:

> Scarcely a man in this section of country is willing to go back to his old command . . . I sent 64 prisoners to Tyler yesterday morning, and will send 13 or more to Maxey in two or three days, and have just heard of 62 deserters in one gang from Maxey's command, and whom I have sent a company of cavalry and sent expresses ahead of them, so that I hope to catch them. The deserters, as far as I know, are not embodied: are in parties of from 4 to 30, and move every two or three days. The party I sent to attack in Denton County got word of our movement and scattered, so that we only got 14 when we should have gotten over 100.

Henry had apparently given up on using Quanrtill to help round up the deserters. As a matter of fact, it seemed that by this date he had given up on Quantrill entirely:

> Quantrill will not obey orders, and so much mischief is charged to his command here that I have determined to disarm, arrest, and send his entire command to you or General Smith. This is the only chance to get them out of this section of country, which they have nearly ruined, and I have never yet got them to do any service. Whenever orders have gone to them they have some excuse, but are certain not to go. In one instance the enrolling officer of Grayson County sent them to impress some whisky at a distillery, under my orders, based upon yours, and they got into a row, killed one man, and plundered the still-house and dwelling, and the next night went back and burned the still-house, but nothing can be proven on them, because the people are afraid to swear against them. They regard the life of a man less than you would that of a sheep-killing dog. My plan now is to arrest Quantrill's men, send you about 100 returned deserters for you to dispose of, and then arrest the balance of the brush crowd, send them to Shreveport, and do all I can to arrest all deserters, those who harbor them, and those who openly avow disloyal sentiments. If the true men of this country would swear what they know I could send several hundred men to the penitentiary for treason & e., but they are afraid and will not make affidavit in any

instance, but I think when I get Quantrill and the brush men out of the way they will have more confidence.

Quantrill and his men are determined never to go into the army or fight in any general battle, first, because many of them are deserters from our Confederate ranks, and next, because they are afraid of being captured, and then because it won't pay men who fight for plunder. I regard them as but one shade better than highwaymen, and the community believe that they have committed all the robberies that have been committed about here for some time, and every man that has any money about his house is scared to death, nearly, and several mon-eyed men have taken their money and gone where they feel more secure.

In this letter to General Magruder, it seemed McCulloch got some things off of his chest that he dared not write to Kirby Smith, who still dreamed of a purpose for the bushwhackers. Then he added: "I am not disposed to complain at my lot, but certainly no other man is surrounded with more difficulties with as little means to meet and overcome them." Then, apparently relieved by the bending of Magruder's ear, he signed his letter with: "Well it is now late at night and I must rest. I will not give up the ship nor 'shorten sail to get off a lee shore,' and nei-ther personal case nor personal danger shall keep me from doing my duty as far as I have the capacity and means, but feel-ing I have but little of either compared to the great demand for both, I can but feel uneasy for my country. For myself I have no care. If I can only see my country free and peace restored I am content."

Two days later, McCulloch wrote to Smith repeating the fact that he did not have the men with enough courage to carry out his orders in regard to the deserters: "Quantrill has not moved a peg, and I have ordered him and his command arrested; got General Maxey to let Col. Stand Watie help Colonel James Bourland do it."

Bourland was known for his ruthless discipline and had even been accused of killing deserters and Federal prisoners.

Then Henry, as in an after thought, said, "What shall I do with them after arresting them?"[3]

It was a question that Henry would not have to worry about

answering, for all his schemes to use, control, or arrest Quantrill's men and, for that matter, most of the brush men, were for naught.

Henry blamed his failure on the citizenry, who were afraid to speak out against Quantrill, and his own soldiers, who seemed to lack the desire to attack the Missourians. He was, at least to some degree, correct in both assumptions.

On February 15, McCulloch wrote again, this time to Smith's assistant, Capt. E. P. Turner, and reported that General Cooper up in Indian Territory had sighted some 200 to 250 Yankees about forty-five miles from Boggy Depot and apparently ready to make an attack on Fort Washita. He ordered Quantrill to take his men from Preston to protect the fort and sent Colonels Bourland and Martin to meet the enemy.

There is no record of Bourland and Quantrill meeting, but it is almost certain that they did. McCulloch was critical of Bourland's methods of punishing deserters, but it must have brought him a glimmer of hope to think about Quantrill being under the command of the strict Bourland. But it probably never happened.

Earlier, on January 11, McCulloch had tried to make Quantrill join in the regular war and had his assistant adjutant-general, P. H. Thomson, send Quantrill orders:

> Captain: The lieutenant general commanding directs me to revoke the orders instructing you to report to Lieutenant General Holmes.
>
> At the time they were issued active operations against the enemy in Arkansas were contemplated, and it was desirable to have all the re-enforcements possible concentrated. The emergency in that quarter has passed, the lieutenant general directs that you proceed as rapidly as possible to the headquarters of Major-General Magruder with your command, where you will immediately be placed in the face of the enemy. You will start as soon as possible, and acknowledge the receipt of this letter.

Since Quantrill had ignored the order to join General Holmes in the fight in Arkansas, there was little chance he would heed this new order to report and be placed in the face of the enemy, but strangely enough, the guerrillas led the attack, driving the Yankees back north and killing a great number of them. They celebrated by going to Sherman and getting drunk.

Henry's woes were just beginning, for in the harsh winter of north Texas, the bushwhackers seemed to begin to develop a new personality. The hatred that filled most of them because of what the Federals and Kansas Jayhawkers had done to their families was still fervent, but a new form of barbaric treatment of their victims was beginning to develop and would blossom in a horrid, glorious finale at a little Missouri town called Centralia.

Some of the veterans of Quantrill's raiders, and probably many of these were the ones who had joined the bushwhackers to avenge atrocities against their families in Missouri, were appalled by the action of some of their clan and began to slip away.

The murder of Sophia's husband was to shatter Quantrill's command into separate segments early in February of 1864.

Major Butt had gone to Sherman and did not return. Sophia searched for him, but it was about a week before his body was found, his emaciated horse beside him.

Fletch Taylor was seen later wearing Butt's watch.

Sophia continued to manage Glen Eden after burying George in Sherman's West Hill Cemetery with a stone that read: "Thou art gone, no more we meet, / No more our longing looks repeat, / Then let me breathe this parting prayer, / The dictate of my bosom's care, / This is of love the final close, / Oh God the fondest last adieu."

The major did not leave her desitute, as her property, including thirty slaves, was valued at $45,400.[4]

Along with the murder of Major Butt, the guerrillas were robbing and killing citizens at will. One Colonel Alexander, who had a farm just south of Sherman, was robbed and killed by Jim Crow Chiles, John Ross, Fletch Taylor, and Andy Walker.

Quantrill was furious about the murder of Butt and was smart enough to realize that continued killing and robbing of Grayson County citizens would quickly wear the guerrillas' welcome mat to northeast Texas very thin.

It was also evident that Quantrill's control over the men had been undermined by Anderson and Fletcher, and even the faithful Todd dreamed of the day when the command would be his.

The cruel little schoolteacher from Ohio, who had led the

most daring and dreaded band of cutthroats in the history of America, was about to be reduced in rank to the husband of the little thirteen-year-old girl he had practically kidnapped, Kate Clarke.

In Grayson County, the good times were coming to an end, and the various factions of the raiders who remained were about to perform the final act of the strange drama of life and death.

CHAPTER 10

The Battle of Caney Creek

Finally the stage was set for the final disintegration of Quantrill's little psuedo-Southern army. Like mighty empires of the past, it was to crumble because of decay from within rather than by being destroyed by a powerful enemy without.

Gregg was gone, an early deserter of the Quantrill guerrilla band; whether by choice or command, his exit temporarily relieved some of the tension.

Another old faithful to leave was Cole Younger. The exact date of his departure from the crumbling command of Quantrill is not known. Younger wrote his memoirs in 1903, but he had a tendency to exaggerate his exploits and his reports are hardly reliable. Cole's adventures in Texas included a romantic fling with Myra Maebelle. Younger's mother had moved to Scyene, Texas, after her home was burned under Ewing's Order No. 11. While visiting his mother, Cole met an old friend from Missouri, John Shirley, and his daughter, Myra, who was sixteen years old. She flirted with all the guerrillas, including the James boys, but it was Cole, she claimed, who fathered her child. Cole denied it.

Myra Maebelle married Sam Starr after the war and changed her name to become the notorious Belle Starr.

Everyone knew, or strongly suspected, that Fletch Taylor had killed Major Butt, and Bill Anderson was still out of sorts because of Quantrill's objection to his pending marriage. On March 3, with M. Y. Brockett officiating, Lt. William T. Anderson and Bush Smith were united in marriage. The marriage certificate was issued on March 2 by S. Bostick, clerk of the County Court of Grayson County. Bostick, however, must not have been present, for Jim Johnson, his deputy clerk, signed the license for him.

There is a scrawled entry on the certificate in front of the name "Bush" that is not readable, but is probably her real first name.

The final split in the guerrillas' unity was shattered after Anderson defied the orders of Quantrill to marry Bush.

Late in March, according to W. L. Potter in the footnotes of Connelley's book, Quantrill returned from a trip to Houston or San Antonio. Since Potter's letters were written at least forty years after the fact, his reports are suspect.

McCulloch had ordered Quantrill to Corpus Christi once, but it was probably a ploy to get him out of the district, at least for a while, and there is no evidence that Quantrill went. If he did, it would be the first order by McCulloch he actually carried out.

Quantrill took this unopportune time to call his men together and tell them that if there was anyone in his command who was guilty of robbing citizens, they should confess and promise never to do it again.

According to Potter:

> . . . if there was a Man in his Command that had been guilty of Robbing any person While in Texas, that if they would come out and ackowledge their guilt & Promise that they Would Never again repeat it & that they were sorry for it, that they could remain in the command the same as ever & He would not Permit them to be punished for it. He also told them that if one of his Men, Was Guilty of committing and depredations on the Property of citizens of Texas, & if they did not acknowledge it then & there, & if it was afterwards Proved against one of them that they Were Guilty of Violating the Law, that he would not shelter them, but Would have them punished to the full extent of the Law, & he would also Expell them from his command.[1]

Of course, they were all guilty.

Vol. B-1
Pg 218

THE STATE OF TEXAS—COUNTY OF GRAYSON.

To Any Judge of the District Court,

CHIEF JUSTICE OF THE COUNTY COURT, ORDAINED MINISTER OF THE GOSPEL, OR JUSTICE OF THE PEACE

IN AND FOR THE COUNTY OF GRAYSON —GREETING.

You are hereby authorized to celebrate the Rites of Matrimony, between Lieut William T Anderson and Miss Bush Smith and make due return to the Clerk of the County Court of said County within sixty days thereafter, certifying your action under this License

This copy of the marriage license of Bill Anderson and Bush Smith proves that they had, in spite of the doubts of some historians, married. Anderson bought a home for his bride at 1312 Cherry Street, where she raised their daughter, Jammie, after Anderson returned to Missouri and was killed in an ambush.
—Courtesy The Red River Historical Museum

Then Quantrill pushed his luck a little too far. He told them if there were any men in his command who did not agree with his methods of commanding, they would be welcome to leave.

Bill Anderson left camp with about twenty (Potter reported eight or nine) of his men after he informed Quantrill they were not guilty of any crimes but were fed up with his command.

Quantrill had Taylor placed under arrest, but he escaped (or was allowed to escape) and, along with Anderson, went to Bonham, where he admitted to General McCulloch that he had killed Major Butt but had done so on the orders of Quantrill. Probably between Fletcher's confession and Bill Anderson telling him every sin Quantrill had ever committed, McCulloch was excited.

Delighted to have a solid charge against Quantrill and an opportunity to rid his district of the troublemakers, McCulloch did very little investigation into Taylor's confession, except to hear Bill Anderson's testimony, which, of course, was tainted, and immediately send word to Mineral Creek that he wanted to see the guerrilla leader at once.

Quantrill must have suspected that there was something sinister in the general's call and departed Mineral Creek with about sixty men, leaving Todd in charge of the few remaining bushwhackers who were loyal to him.

Todd's loyalty, however, may have been based on the realization that he would soon be the leader of the rebel band.

Connelley states in *Quantrill and the Border Wars* that "Quantrill felt his power slipping away from him and knew that it was going to Todd. He lost his bold independence of demeanor and action, and his attitude towards Todd became subservient, conciliatory, and sometimes pitiably truculent, humble and imploring."

In was near the end of the month of March 1864, and the end of Quantrill's command was fast approaching.

The guerrilla leader must have known, or at least strongly suspected, that Fletcher and Anderson had been bending McCulloch's ear and that trouble awaited him in Bonham, although McCulloch had told him he had Taylor under arrest and wanted to hear Quantrill's charges against him.

Upon his arrival, the guerrilla chief was escorted to McCulloch's room at the City Hotel.

Henry explained that he did, indeed, have Taylor under arrest but revealed that he had implicated Quantrill in the murder of Butt and that he was a prisoner.

McCulloch then invited Quantrill to go to the hotel dining room and have dinner with him.

W. L. Potter, in his letters to W. W. Scott, quoted Quantrill, who must have been livid when he discovered Taylor's deception, as saying: "No sir, I will not. I consider this a strange way of doing business Gen. McCullough [*sic*]. I do not understand your manner of doing business Gen. McCullough. I have preferred a criminal charge against one of My officers. I have Placed him under Guard as you Well Know. He made his Escape from my Camp, and now you place me under arrest on his Word and undertake to try me for the crime that he acknowledges that he committed. No Sir. I will not go to Dinner. By God, I do not Care a God Damn if I never taste another mouthful on this Earth."

This statement appears in the footnotes of Connelly's book. However, Potter was in Dallas when the event took place, so his report is secondhand at best, and in many other statements, Potter is proved to be unreliable.

In any event, McCulloch went to dinner, leaving the distraught bushwhacker commander in the room under guard by two privates of Martin's Texas Regiment.

Quantrill's navy revolvers lay on the bed, and on the pretense of getting a drink of water, he grabbed the pistols and forced the guards to lay down their arms.

At the bottom of the stairs, he met two more guards, whom he disarmed, and ran into the street, shouting to his men that it was a trap.

The sixty men still faithful to him dashed down the streets of Bonham and headed for the safety of Mineral Creek, perhaps forty miles away.

When McCulloch got word of the escape, which interrupted his dinner, he sent Col. J. Martin's regiment in pursuit. Martin's command was the Fifth Texas Partisan Rangers, who had been ordered to Bonham on October 9, 1863, by General Steele, who stated: "The exigencies of the service require the use of these troops temporarily in that district."[2] Six months must have seemed like a very long "temporary" service to Martin.

Now the crack in the guerrillas' unity became a chasm as Bill Anderson and his men joined Martin and the legitimate Confederate soldiers in the chase.

A brief but heated battle took place at a little creek between Bonham and Sherman.

Leslie, in *The Devil Knows How To Ride,* reports that the fight occurred on Bodark Creek, but there are two problems with that assumption. First, the name of the creek, and the tree, in Texas is spelled *bois d'arc*, a reminder that some of the early explorers of the territory had been French. The wood of the tree is very hard and will cast off sparks if placed on a campfire.

The work *Bodark* appears in the letters of W. L. Potter. The only problem is, no matter how you spell it, the creek is on the east and south sides of Bonham, and from there it runs in a westerly direction; it hardly seems likely that Quantrill would have ridden out the wrong side of town and then circled back to head toward Sherman.

In Connelly's *Quantrill and the Border Wars,* which is heavily footnoted, he quotes Potter as saying, "I think it was Bodark creek, if not, it was a stream called Caney." Caney Creek is located on the west side of Bonham and is much more likely to be the place where the bushwhackers began to shoot at each other.

For Quantrill to have crossed Bois d'Arc Creek, he would have had to ride out of Bonham for several miles and then turn back east on a direct route to Colbert's Ferry.

Grayson County historian Tony Swindill believes that Quantrill did not take a direct route to Colbert's Ferry but rode southwest out of Bonham to Kentuckytown for fresh horses. To reach Kentuckytown from Bonham, the raiders would certainly have had to cross Bois d'Arc Creek, which wraps around Bonham in a southwesterly direction. That is possible, since riding horses for the thirty to forty miles to Mineral Creek or Colbert's Ferry would have depleted them, and with the guerrillas mounted on fresh horses, the troops chasing them would have been slowed to a walk.

It that is true, then Quantrill probably went back to Mineral

Creek camp before heading for the Red River the next day. Todd and his men still could have met Anderson at Caney Creek for the shootout.

Bill Anderson led the guerrillas in pursuit of their formal leader, joining Colonel Martin and his militia. Potter reports the number to be "several hundred," but his estimates are usually exaggerated.

Regardless of the numbers involved, it had to be the most unusual engagement of the Civil War, with rebellious, undisciplined, guerrillas under Anderson joining with the prim, military Colonel Martin to chase their own kind across north Texas.

Since casualties were extremely low, one has to wonder how seriously the sharp-shooting Missourians took the conflict with their brother guerrillas.

Some reports say that Quantrill and some of his men went back to Mineral Creek and left Todd to fight the rear-guard action, but indications are that he headed directly for the Red River and sanctuary in Indian Territory.

In *The Devil Knows How to Ride,* Leslie states that Quantrill sent a rider on a race horse[3] to Mineral Creek to get Todd with the message that he planned to head directly to Colbert's Ferry and to meet him on the Sherman-Bonham road. If that is true, it reinforces the speculation that the battle took place on Caney Creek, not Bois d'Arc.

Regardless of the location, before they could meet, Quantrill and his men were driven from the road by the pursuers and turned north toward the ferry.

Todd, according to Leslie, ran into Anderson and his men, who had given up the chase, and after firing at each other and one man was slightly wounded.

The fueding guerrillas did more than sling bullets, as Todd and Anderson had a verbal exchange.

"If you are not a damned set of cowards," Anderson yelled, "come out into the open and fight like men."

"You have the most men," Todd replied. "If you are not a set of God damn cowards, come in here and take us."

There was another round of shooting, but no one was hit, and Todd withdrew to head for the Red, where he joined his colonel.[4]

This version of the event coincides with the report of W. L. Potter in the notes of Connelley's *Quantrill and the Border Wars:*

> Todd was on the same road that he was ordered to come, it was some five Miles East of Sherman, on the Bonham Road, that he met Anderson With some 12 0r fourteen men. He may have had more. He had some of col Martin's men with him at that time. at all events he out numbered Todd. In the Mean time Quantrill had been compelled to abandon that Road & Was slowly Retreating on the Road to colbert's Ferry on Red River, a few Miles North of the Sherman & Bonham road. Todd heard the firing and Kept along the timber of the creek. I now think it was Bodark creek. if not, it was a stream called caney.

However they traveled, when they arrived the guerrillas under Quantrill were joined by Todd and his men on the north side of the river.

The far side of the Red River, bristling with the guns of the bushwhackers, gave Colonel Martin cause to reflect, and after a meeting with Quantrill in the middle of the river under a flag of truce, he determined that, at least on this day, his jurisdiction ended on the south side of the river. He returned with his men to Bonham.

Anderson and his men hung around, and deep in the night they crossed the river and kidnapped Andy Walker, one of Quantrill's men. They tried to steal Quantrill's horse, Old Charley, but the horse, which only Quantrill could ride, put up such a fuss that they abandoned the scheme.

The disintegration of the most feared band of marauders in history was complete.

Todd was now in command of what was left of the men faithful to Quantrill, and they headed north. There had been heavy spring rains and river crossings were dangerous, and somewhere along the trail, the division between Todd and Quantrill also deepened and widened.

Quantrill would renew his affair with Kate and hide out in the brush of west Missouri. He would emerge only to play a minor role in Sterling Price's final folly, the invasion of Missouri, before heading for Kentucky and his death.

Anderson and his group also headed home and would bring new disgrace to the Southern cause they pretended to espouse: their inhumane action at Centralia, where innocent prisoners were shot down and their bodies mutilated.

Of all the players in the sequence of events, the killer Fletch Taylor survived in style. After the war he became a wealthy lead miner at Joplin, but his name could still strike fear in the heart of W. L. Potter, who wrote: "I would rather his name would not appear in connection with the Major Butt affair, & especially have me as the authority for it."[5]

But the most feared name in the history of the Civil War, William Clarke Quantrill, would appear in only one final scene. He would soon be reduced to a crippled and dying icon, and would, in his last days, express his own fear by embracing God.

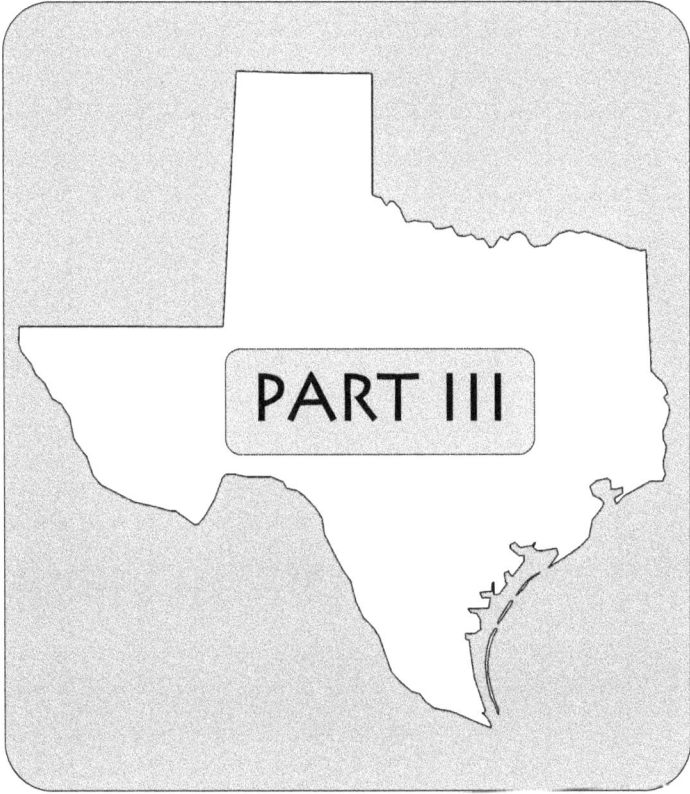

PART III

CHAPTER 11

The Bushwhacker Turns Savage

Finally the madness, at least as far as Texas was concerned, had come to an end. As McCulloch breathed a sigh of relief down in Bonham, the Federal military forces in Missouri must have been hyperventilating as reports came that the bushwhackers, though divided, were headed back to their state.

The dreaded Quantrill, subdued possibly to the point of depression, went into a self-imposed exile with his bride Kate Clarke, in Howard County. A few faithful, namely James Little, John Barker, John Ross, Allen Parmer, Frank James, and David Hilton, remained faithful to their fallen leader.

Todd was leading his own group, and Clements and Anderson were about to commit an act that would make Lawrence and Baxter Springs look like Sunday school picnics.

Sterling Price began his bungled invasion of Missouri in the fall of 1864 and had called on the guerrillas to take part by harassing the enemy and destroying railroad tracks and communication lines.

Once again, the noble Price compromised his values and tried to find a useful purpose for the useless bushwhackers. It was the act of a desperate leader grasping for straws in a collapsing haystack.

The story of Centralia, Missouri, is not part of the history of Quantrill's men in Texas but is told here to illustrate the level of inhumanity to which the guerrillas had sunk. Somewhere in

Texas, they had lost their last shred of decency and adopted the tactics of the most vicious predator. No longer were they Robin Hoods of Sherwood Forest or avenging angels but had become bloodthirsty and extremely sadistic.

One probable cause of the new wave of inhumane predications by the raiders was that Quantrill was no longer in charge. Bill Anderson's reins were woven of human hair. There had been scalping and mutilations of bodies on a lesser scale, but the vile acts committed on innocents, particularly by Anderson and Clements, surpassed anything that had been done before, either by the guerrillas or Federal authorities, or, for that matter, by John Brown in his heyday of butchering slaveholders.

The split-up of the bushwhackers had very little effect on the citizens of Sherman but gave rise to devastating results when they got back to Missouri.

On the morning of September 27, Bloody Bill Anderson rode into Centralia. Todd remained with some of the men in camp. They were, as the crow flies, at least 150 miles from the little earthenworks called Fort Davidson where Price's army of 12,000 men was being repelled by 900 Federal troops.

If the guerrillas were destroying communications and railroads, their actions were too far away from Price to do him any good, although Anderson had presumably ridden into town to find out news about Price's whereabouts.

Anderson's men robbed the stores and stole bolts of cloth and women's shoes. At a storage depot, they broke open all the crates and, as luck would have it, found, along with four cases of boots, their favorite loot, a barrel of whiskey.

In almost every case of guerrilla depredations on the populace, they were drunk.

A train arrived with Federal soldiers on board, headed home on furlough. They were removed from the train and forced to strip to their underwear.

At Anderson's command, Clements and his men "paroled" them. Most of them received several wounds, but all had one thing in common: a bullet hole in the forehead.

J. Thomas Fyfer, in his *History of Boone County, Missouri* (St. Louis: Western Historical Company, 1882) best describes what happened:

A dozen of the prisoners, shot through the brain or the heart, fell dead at the first volley. Others screamed and staggered about with a hand pressed to their wounds until, shot again and again, they tumbled lifeless to the ground . . . Others wandered about, stunned and bleeding, and in their agony staggered against the very muzzles of the revolvers of the guerrillas. One or two started for the railroad and fell dead within a few feet of it. Some cried, "O, God, have mercy!" but most of them merely groaned and moaned in the most agonizing manner . . . One man lay on his back with his hands clenched tightly in the short grass. Another lay with one bullet-hole over the eye, another in his face, a third in his breast. He was unconscious, his eyes were closed, he did not moan, but, with a sort of spasmodic motion, he dragged his right heel on the ground, back and forth. "He's marking time," said Arch Clement, jocosely.

Edward Leslie, in *The Devil Knows How to Ride,* gives an excellent account of the Centralia massacre, and the only purpose for mentioning it here is to show the depths of debauchery to which the guerrillas had lowered themselves.

Maj. A.V.E. Johnston and the 39th Missouri Infantry Volunteers, in service for two weeks and untested in the field, arrived at Centralia and rode after the renegades and, unfortunately, caught up with them.

Stupidly dismounted, they faced the guerrillas, who could not believe their good fortune, and charged the volunteers. The troops got off one volley, and one of the bullets struck Frank Shepherd in the head, his blood and brains splattering on Frank James, who was riding beside him.

The guerrillas called for the surrender of the militia after surrounding them, and a new slaughter was about to begin.

Sturgeon, September 29, 1864

After leaving Centralia on Tuesday the guerrillas fell back about two miles to the timber, keeping pickets in view of the town. Major Johnston was then following their trail with 150 men. He went to where they were, and when he came in sight dismounted his men and formed them in line, each man holding his own horse. The guerrillas were moving toward him but checked up at this, but soon came on a charge. When 150 yards distant the major ordered his men to fire, which they did, bringing the enemy to a halt. After the volley they came on, and when within 100 yards, the men began to break, many of them not firing the second shot, and none of them more than that. It then became a scene of murder and outrage at which the heart sickens. Most of them were beaten over the head, seventeen of them were scalped, and one man had his privates cut off and placed in his mouth. Every man was shot in the head. One man had his nose cut off. One hundred and fifty dead bodies have been found, including four taken from the train. I moved to Centralia yesterday, and knowing that Douglas and Major King were somewhere in the country toward which Anderson is supposed to have taken, I did not follow. I endeavored in every way to find out their whereabouts, but have not been able to hear of them since they went into that country. Anderson was at least thirty hours ahead of me when I got to Centralia, and I know he must turn back or cross the river before I could get to him. I came back here, after ordering the citizens to bury the eighty-five bodies left at Centralia, as this was the best point at which to get information from the country. Colonel Stauber sent out scouts this afternoon, which have not yet returned, to ascertain the cause of firing heard by citizens of the country south of this. The party has orders not to fight, but get information. As soon as it returns I will give results.

   Dan. M. Draper
   Lieutenant Colonel.[1]

Centralia, with all its horrors, was eclipsed here in the enormity and infamous conduct of the bloody demons. At least one wounded man was castrated, and his genitals stuffed into his mouth. Men's heads were severed from their lifeless bodies, exchanged as to bodies, labeled with rough and obscene epitaphs . . . stuck on their carbine points, tied to their saddle bows, or grinning at each other from the tops of fence stakes and stumps around the scene.[2]

It was obvious that when Quantrill lost control of the men, they became obsessed by their most base instincts. They had scalped men before, but in the summer and early fall of 1864, it seemed that at least some of them went completely mad.

In Carroll County, Anderson's men were attacked by citizens, and during the fight John Maupin not only shot John Kirker but scalped him and sawed off his head.

In the same fight, Anderson shot Mrs. Stephen Mitchell as she tried to escape. The incident even turned the stomach of Fletch Taylor, who left Anderson to ride with Thrailkill.

In a fight on Fayette Road, two militiaman, named John W. Daniels and John Nichols, were killed. As the *Missouri Statesman* reported: "From the forehead of Daniels a round portion of skin had been cut about the size of a Mexican dollar, and from that of Nichols a longer piece was taken from the center of the forehead to the region of the left temple." A note was attached to Daniels' clothing: "You come to hunt bushwhackers. Now you ar skelpt. Clenyent skept you. Wm. Anderson."

The bushwhackers had always respected "decent" women, making whores and young slavegirls the target of their sexual pleasures, but not only did Anderson shoot Mrs. Mitchell, but he threatened bodily harm to others, probably still burning inside because of what the Federals had done to his sisters in Kansas City.

When Gen. Egbert Brown arrested some Southern women and Miss Anna Fickle of Warrenburg was convicted of attempting to aid a Confederate prisoner in escaping and sentenced to three years, Anderson sent Brown a note:

"I do not like the idea of warring with women and children, but if you do not release all the women you have arrested in La Fayette County, I will hold the Union ladies in the county as hostages for them. I will tie them by the neck in the brush and starve them until they are released, if you do not release them. The ladies of Warrensburg must have Miss Fickle released. I hold them responsible for her speedy and safe return. General, do not think I am jesting with you. I will resort to abusing your ladies if you do not quit imprisoning ours."

Although the threat was never carried out, the tone of the message indicated that the bushwhackers had departed from the tradition that women, except for blacks and prostitutes, were sacred.

Anderson's actions have been justified by some because of what the Federals did to his sisters, and there is no doubt the artrocities committed by Federal authority were horrible and he had good cause to hate them, but obviously something had snapped in Anderson's already-deviant mind.

Once again, the demonic savagery of the bushwhacker had moved north to whence it began and the citizens of Missouri, along with the Federal troops stationed there, were to taste the bloodthirsty revenge, amplified to the point of madness.

And down in Texas, the residents of Grayson County could only rejoice that it was not happening to them. But they had problems of their own, not made by guerrilla hands.

CHAPTER 12

Sherman After the War

With the exodus of the guerrillas in the spring of 1864, the residents of Sherman and Grayson County should have been able to breathe a sigh of relief and hope that life would return to normal.

The problem was, it did return to normal and the same old conflicts were still in their midst. The distrust of neighbors that had led to the great Gainesville hanging, the hundreds of brush men still hiding out in Jernigan and Wildcat thickets, and the lawlessness did not go north with the bushwhackers.

Although most of the Missourians went north, a few remained in Texas, and even more were to return after the war.

McCulloch may have been pleased when word came that the raiders were headed north, but it was a short-lived respite.

As the circumstances of the Southern cause worsened, the crowd hiding out in Jerrigan's Swamp and closer to home, Wildcat Thicket, which spanned the Grayson–Fannin county line, began to grow.

In the fall of 1863, McCulloch had formed the "Brush Battalion," made up of about seven hundred men who had emerged from the thickets. His purpose for them was to fight Indians and hunt down their fellow deserters, still living in the brush.

Henry should have learned his lesson with Quantrill; his recruits soon began to perform poorly, "committing petty depre-

dations on the property of the people about all their camps."
Soon most of the deserters rejoined the ranks in the thicket, and
the battalion was disbanded in March of 1864.[1]

McCulloch wrote a letter about the battalion of brush men,
his tone suggestive of despair:

> . . . There is not one bit of reliability in the deserters that
> have returned to service up here as a mass; here and there a
> good man, generally bad, and steps must be taken to put the
> last one of them into his former command, the grave, or
> prison. To do this I must have more force, and the sooner 'tis
> done the better.
>
> The brush command are deserting constantly and going
> back to the brush or to the Federals . . . I have never been in a
> country where the people were so perfectly worthless and so
> cowardly as here. I am now trying as a last resort to get them
> to organize a company in each county for police duty. If I can
> effect this in time to root out the men in the brush before
> spring I may save the country; otherwise it will go up certain if
> the Federals make any demonstrations. I would like to get out
> of this country, I assure you, but am unwilling to ask to be al-
> lowed to leave a sinking ship.

In January of 1864, Col. James Bourland received a letter
from J. W. Hale of Decatur:

> Dear Sir:
> Permit me to drop you a few lines in regard to the state of af-
> fairs in our country. We of the frontier portion of this country
> are thrown in a state of the most wild excitement. It is gener-
> ally believed that we are on the very eve of an insurrection and
> that the secession portion of our population are daily in great
> danger of being jayhawked by Fox and his outlawed gang, as-
> sociated with the Indians. If something cannot be speedily ac-
> complished to our relief, all the true Southern men in this por-
> tion of the country will leave with their families for the more
> thickly inhabited portion of the State, which will have only the
> effect of weakening the frontier. Some speedy and effective
> movement of the troops here to our protection will be the only
> means of saving this portion of the frontier. I confess that I am

incompetent to suggest any plan of operation, but sincerely hope that your better judgment will devise some means to save our country from ruin and check the torrent of blood that is daily threatening to deluge our once happy country. Speedy and effective operations is our only hope for our country's salvation. There have some things developed that I do not feel at liberty to write.

Bourland, along with McCulloch, must have wished that citizen Hale could have suggested a solution for how to carry out "speedy and effective operations."

Things were not going to get any better for the beleaguered Confederate command in northeast Texas, for not only did the brush keep filling up with new deserters and the Federals keep threatening an invasion, but on the frontier the Indians became more active, pushing back the edge of the frontier one hundred miles during the war.

Finally the war came to a close, and with the Federal victory, it was soon evident that the tables had turned in northeast Texas.

Those who had voted against secession and survived, or who hadn't returned to their homes in Kansas, were now in charge, for all Southern sympathizers were removed from office.

In 1867, the Grayson County officers were: J. D. George, county judge; J. G. Owens, clerk; R. M. Smith, sheriff; J. W. Hunter, deputy.

All of them had taken an oath swearing that they had not voluntarily borne arms against the United States and that they would support and defend the U.S. Constitution:

> I, ——— do solemnly swear (or affirm) that I have never voluntarily borne arms against the United States since I have been a citizen thereof; that I have voluntarily given no aid, countenance, counsel, or encouragement to persons engaged in armed hostility thereto; that I have neither sought nor accepted, nor attempted to exercise the functions of any office whatever, under any authority or pretended authority, in hostility to the United States; that I have not yielded a voluntary support to any pretended government, authority, power, or

constitution within the United States, hostile or inimical thereto. And I do further swear that, to the best of my knowledge and ability, I will support the defend the Constitution of the United States against all enemies, foreign and domestic; that I will bear true faith and allegiance to the same; that I take this obligation freely, without any mental reservation or purpose of evasion, and that I will well and faithfully discharge the duties of the office on which I am about to enter, so help me God.

The Freedmen's Bureau did not begin operations in Texas until December of 1965, and former slaves gathered in the streets of Sherman, uncertain as to their status or future.

The returning Confederate veterans, who straggled home as best they could, found that they had very little left in the way of material possessions and they were denied the right to bear arms.

They were not allowed to vote, either, and in an election held on February 10, 1868, Federal soldiers watched the polling places to be sure no Confederate veteran voted, although the newly freed slaves were encouraged to cast their votes, thus ensuring that the new Texas constitution would be written by negroes and radical men from the north.

Many of the troops sent to Grayson County to enforce the terms of surrender were colored, and reports of women "walking the plank" to be stripped of their clothing and even openly raped, without impunity, were rampant.

In his memoirs, a little paper entitled "When the Yankee Soldiers Made a Run For Safety," Capt. J. E. Carraway wrote:

"At every county seat there was an assemblage of Yankee soldiers and sometimes they were negroes, who to us were equally obnoxious. But we were taking our medicine. There was no recourse. We had no Government to appeal to for aid or redress. The die had been cast, and we among the unfortunate. In the meantime the Ku Klux Klan was born from necessity and meant for use under conditions necessitous. It lived a time, filled the niche designed, and then went into oblivion and history."[2]

And the fighting was far from over. The guns of war had not even cooled before they were reheated in personal vengenge, revenge, and family feuds, such as the Lee–Peacock feud at four corners.

The frontier was left unprotected, since not only the returning soldiers but the populace who supported them barred from bearing arms. Outlying ranches and farms became easy prey for Indians, outlaws, and renegade whites and negroes.

On February 3, 1866, the *Dallas Herald* reported: "We are informed that some weeks since, the military authorities in Grayson County arrested a man by the name of Poindexter, charged with murder, during the war, of some one whose name has not been learned. They also arrested two other persons whose names are not recollected by our informant, charged with robbery and murder, committed in that country some two years ago."

It was a time when those who had opposed secession from the Union had their day in court, and the courts were all stacked in their favor.

The killings were numerous, and many of them unrecorded, but it was obvious the shoe was now on the other foot. Many of those who had hidden in Jernigan Thicket to avoid Confederate conscription now came out to regain their proper place in the pro-Union society of Grayson County.

Texas had, for the most part, escaped the destruction of war such as occurred in the east and particularly in the path of Sherman's devastating march to the sea.

Many refugees from the South began to load their belongings on wagons and head for the promised land of Texas, where there was still lots of space and fewer carpetbaggers and Federal troops, they hoped.

Not only outlaws and guerrillas but many honest southerners carved the initials "GTT" (for "Gone to Texas," a slogan that would become the title of the book from which the movie *The Outlaw Josey Wales* was made) on their porch post and headed south or west.

Sherman continued to grow, and by the late 1860s it was the most important city in northeast Texas, its marketplace crowded with cotton wagons waiting to unload, wagons filled with potatoes and watermelons in season, and wagon trains loaded with as many as 80,000 green bison hides.

By 1870, the migration to Texas had reached new heights, and a citizen of Clarksville reported that he had seen 130 wagons crossing the Canadian River, all headed for Sherman and the promised land of Texas.

In 1872, farm property in Grayson County was valued from $4 to $15 per acre.

And what effect had the Missourians had on the town and the county?

Very little, unless you were Sophia Butt, looking for a new husband, or Bush Anderson, raising your fatherless little girl named Jimmye in the little house at 1312 Cherry Street. Or if you were the steeple on the Methodist church.

The merchants of Sherman, except for the Iron Post Grocery, were glad to have customers who actually paid for their goods.

For the most part, the scars left on Sherman by the bandits from up north were temporary and did heal, albeit it sometimes slowly. But Sherman was not to escape the return of some of the raiders, who found their homes burned in Missouri, or maybe even a price on their head and a multitude of Pinkerton detectives on their trail.

With their little sister married and teaching school in Sherman, Frank and Jesse James were frequent visitors in Sherman and in McKinney, where they had friends. Allen Parmer moved to Alpine before passing away in Wichita Falls in 1927.

David Poole settled in Sherman after the war, and J. Frank Dalton, who claimed he was Jesse James, died in Granbury in 1951.

In Austin after the war, George Shepherd slit the throat of James Anderson on the lawn of the state capitol. The younger brother of Bloody Bill had, along with Jesse James, murdered Shepherd's nephew, Ike Flannery, for his inheritance.

Today the city of Sherman is a bustling county seat with a wide band of concrete, Highway 75, running south to the metropolis of Dallas or north a short distance to the Red River and Oklahoma, where you can cross on a bridge instead of Colbert's Ferry.

In the 1940s, work was begun on Lake Texoma by the Corps

of Engineers by impounding the waters of the Red River on 89,000 acres, which inundated the site of Glen Eden and many of the haunts of the guerrillas. Sophia's home was dismantled in the 1940s, with each board carefully numbered so it could be re-assembled outside the confines of Lake Texoma, but some soldiers, camping in the area, used the lumber for firewood.

Preston Cemetery is still there, with the graves of Holland Coffee and Sophia, who was buried in pink satin. Her last husband, James Porter, rests with her inside the iron fence that surrounds their unkept graves, while Holland is on the outside, his grave moved from its former site.

Standing on the square in Sherman today, the only reminder of the war is the first Confederate monument in Texas, erected on April 3, 1896. There is a marker at 404 West Washington Street, marking the path of the Butterfield Stage, and out at Preston, a granite marker stands where Coffee's Indian Trading Post was founded in 1837.

Visit Sherman and you won't hear the sound of Ben Smith's hammer ringing on the anvil, or the raucous roars of the drunks at the Iron Post Grocery. The sweet smell of Wagoner's bakery won't tempt you with the promise of pies and cakes for ten cents, and the big red store won't offend you with its brashness.

But if you stand on the square in Sherman and listen closely, you might hear the Rebel yell coming from the throats of the drunken raiders as they ride through, their reins in their mouths and two navy Colts firing wildly in the air.

What Ever Happened To...?

For a few of the guerrillas, the end of the war was also the end of their pseudomilitary career. They went home to their families and farms and resumed a normal lifestyle, hindered by Federal rules and carpetbagger diplomacy.

Others never seemed to find a way to let go of the guerrilla image and became thieves, robbers, and murderers without a cause.

Because of their wartime activities, many of the bushwhackers were hunted men, if not by law enforcement then by the relatives of the men they had killed or robbed during the war.

The Pinkerton Agency, developed during the war, became involved in hunting down reformed Rebels such as Sam Hildebrand, who finally moved to Texas to escape the mighty arm of the law.

Unfortunately, the reasons many of them fought with Quantrill were still there, and the disputes with neighbors and even family members did not stop with the end of the war.

And many of them found peace only in death, either during the remainder of the war, or in violence of a less organized nature.

And some, such as Quantrill and Jesse James, could not even find peace in death. Jesse was reported alive by men who claimed to be the Robin Hood of American history, and a report that Quantrill was living in Canada after the war prompted one musuem to take his bones off display.

The folowing is a summary of how the guerrillas lived, or died.

BLOODY BILL ANDERSON

Acting Lt. Col. Samuel P. Cox received a tip from a woman that Anderson and his men were camped out in the vicinity of Albany, Missouri, and on October 27, 1864, Cox accomplished his assignment of destroying the guerrilla chieftain. A young man from Kentucky, Cox had special orders from General Craig to "find and whip Anderson."

It was just about a month after the Centralia fiasco, and public opinion was very inflamed about the artrocities the raiders had committed there.

Cox, who had studied guerrilla tactics, decided to use them himself against the raiders. At noon he arrived at Albany. Leaving every fourth man in his command in the town, he took the rest about four hundred yards south and deployed them on a narrow lane.

He then sent a detachment of men to find and engage the guerrillas, with orders to fall back. The old bushwhacker trick of pulling a force into an ambush was about to be used against Anderson, with devastating results.

One Union officer wrote in his diary that time seemed to stand still until the detachment came charging back, the bush-whackers in hot pursuit, yelling like madmen.

The Union line simply opened up and let them ride through, and at a range of one hundred yards they sprayed the guerrillas with a deadly fire. The raiders were in complete disarray and confusion as they returned the fire of their tormentors.

Finally, two riders rode toward the Union line at full gallop. One rider, astride a great gray horse, had the reins in his teeth and was firing two revolvers. He fell in a hail of bullets and his companion toppled to the ground and crawled into the brush.

When the soldiers approached the first man, they found that two bullets had torn into the side of his head. Beside his body was a white hat with a long black plume stuck in the brim. He wore a frock coat and blue vest and the usual embroidered shirt of the guerrillas.

In his pockets they found almost $600 and a hank of blond hair, along with a photo of a woman and a letter signed, "your ever loving and obedient wife until death—Bush Anderson—at home Friday evening, April 20th, 1864." It also mentioned "some toys for her babe." There was also a lock of fine dark chestnut brown hair.

Then they found a small Confederate flag with the inscription "Presented to W. L. Anderson by his friend, F.M.R. Let it not be contaminated by Fed. hands." Two sheets of paper were also on the body: General Sterling Price's order to "Captain Anderson," dated October 11.

The body was duly photographed (ambrotypes) and displayed. It was finally buried in a shallow grave in the cemetery on the outskirts of town where, that evening, militiamen spat and urinated on it.

John Edwards reported in his *Noted Guerrillas* that Anderson kept a silken cord, tying a knot in it each time he killed a man. The cord was not found on his body but supposedly appeared later with fifty-three knots in it.

Back in Sherman, Texas, Bush Anderson sat in her home at 1312 Cherry Street and rocked her female infant, Jimmye, who was the result of her brief encounter with the rebel guerrilla known as Bloody Bill. It had been about eight months since he had ridden north and left her.

She was not aware that one of the soldiers had cut off her husband's ring finger in order to steal their wedding band. According to Carl Breihan, they also cut off his head, which was placed on a pole and left there for some time.

Like Jesse James and Quantrill, Anderson was rumored to be alive and living in Brownwood, Texas, after the war, along with Henry Ford, who some thought was Jesse James.[1]

It is ironic that in a life so wasted as that of Bill Anderson, they could not even get the date of birth correct on his tombstone.

Official Records of the War of the Rebellion, Series 1, Vol. XLI
Part 1, page 442:
Report of Lieut. Col. Samuel P. Cox, Thirty-third Infantry
Enrolled Missouri Militia.
Richmond, Mo., October 27, 1864

Dear Sir: We have the honor to report the result of our expedition on yesterday against the notorious bushwhacker, William T. Anderson and his forces, near Albany, in the southwest corner of this county (Ray).

Learning his whereabouts we struck camp on yesterday morning and made a forced march and came in contact with their pickets about a mile this side of Albany; drove them in and through Albany and into the woods beyond. We dismounted our men in the town, threw our infantry force into the woods beyond, sending a cavalry advance who engaged the enemy and fell back, when Anderson and his fiendish gang, about 300 strong, raised the Indian yell and came in full speed upon our lines, shooting and yelling as they came. Our lines held their position without a break. The notorious bushwhacker, Anderson, and one of his men, supposed to be Captain Rains, son of General Rains, charged through our lines. Anderson was killed and fell some fifty steps in our rear, receiving balls in the side of the head. Rains made his escape and their forces retreated in full speed, being completely routed; one cavalry pursued them some ten miles, finding the road strewn with blood for miles. We hear of them scattered in various directions, some considerable force of them making their way toward Richfield, in Clay County. We captured on Anderson private papers and orders from General Price that identify him beyond a doubt.

I have the honor to report that my officers and men conducted themselves well and fought bravely on the field. We had 4 men wounded; lost none. The forces of my command consisted of a portion of Major Grimes', of Ray County, Fifty-first Regiment Enrolled Missouri Militia, and a portion of the Thirty-third Enrolled Missouri Militia, from Daviess [*sic*] and Caldwell Counties.

Respectively, yours, S. P. Cox
Lieut. Col. Comdg. Thirty-third
Regt. Enrolled Missouri Militia.[2]

JOHN MCCORKLE

McCorkle's parole was issued at Newcastle, Kentucky, where he had gone with Quantrill, and after the chieftain's death, McCorkle stayed in Kentucky and farmed for a short time.

He returned to Missouri and was married in 1867, espousing the Baptist faith and finishing out his life peacefully. He passed away on January 18, 1918, at the age of seventy-nine and was buried in Lisbon, Missouri.

McCorkle, in writing *Three Years with Quantrill*, glossed over many of the guerrilla leader's faults. Much as Sam Hildebrand did in his confessions, McCorkle may have had an interest in what history would think of their exploits.

JESSE JAMES

In looking at the life of Jesse James, the question that comes to mind is: "Will the real Jesse James please stand up?" He was just a teenager, too young to ride with Quantrill at Lawrence, who became the most beloved, or most hated, person in the country.

The Robin Hood image that was awarded him, by pulp novels and by John Edwards, was hardly the real Jesse. Neither was he a cruel, sadistic killer, as were some of the men who rode with Quantrill. He was, as most of the guerrillas were, an enigma.

The Hollywood image of a swashbuckling hero played by Tyrone Power, with Henry Fonda as Frank, was planted in the minds of many. These fictional James brothers robbed from evil banks and railroads and helped those they had oppressed. Perhaps the worst movie made on the subject starred Audie Murphy as Jesse and a paunchy, middle-aged Brian Donlevy, dressed in full Confederate uniform, as Quantrill.

A recent movie, *American Outlaws*, is a farce that will probably give the present generation a warped image of what the outlaw was really like, and another, *Ride with the Devil*, was a box-office bomb.

There were those who rose up in later years to announce that they were the real Jesse James, reincarnated from the grave or brush and living in Missouri caves or on Texas farms.

The real Jesse tried to surrender at Lexington but was shot in May or June of 1865. To nurse him back to health, his mother took him to Kansas City to the home of her uncle, John Mimms. Here he met and fell in love with his cousin, Zerelda, who was called Zee.

After his recovery, he and brother Frank, along with the Younger brothers, formed the James–Younger gang, which was to terrorize Missouri banks and railroads. Their first bank robbery was the Clay County Savings Bank in Liberty.

When they robbed the Kansas City fairgrounds in 1872 with thousands of fair attendees on the grounds, the writer John Edwards began to glorify the gang as "Robin Hoods," giving them "a halo of medieval chivalry upon their garments" and claiming they had "shown us how the things were done that poets sing of."

Protected by the citizenry and hounded by Pinkerton agents, they seemed to float across the landscape, robbing a bank, a stagecoach, or a train with impunity and dashing heroism.

Late in January of 1875, Pinkerton men, thinking Frank and Jesse were home, threw a bomb into the house, killing their young half-brother, Archie Samuels, and injuring their mother's hand, causing her to have her arm amputated later. The agents claimed they had thrown a railroad flare that unfortunately landed in the fireplace and exploded.

After a disaster in Northfield, Minnesota, in September of 1876 in which the Younger brothers were wounded and captured and Jesse and Frank barely escaped, Jesse, who had married Zee in 1874, changed his name to Howard and went into hiding.

Governor Thomas J. Crittenden had placed a reward on Jesse of $5,000, and on April 3, 1882, Robert Ford shot Jesse in the back of the head as he was straightening a picture on the wall.

Claims that it was not Jesse killed by "the dirty little coward, who shot Mr. Howard, and put Jesse James in his grave" have been numerous, but recent investigations have reinforced the fact that Jesse James is buried in Kearney, Missouri.

SAM HILDEBRAND

It was a very private war. So private that it would not end when Lee, or even Kirby Smith, surrendered. From the beginning, Sam Hildebrand's hatred for unionists was not motivated by a love of the South, a desire to maintain the institution of slavery, or even a belief in the rights of states to govern themselves.

Sam's war was against those who had done him wrong and everyone else who might be remotely connected to them. The vigilantes who killed his brothers and burned his home were his enemies, and since they seemed to be on the side of the North, the Federal soldiers, particularly if they were of Dutch descent, were included on his hate list.

After the war, Sam tried to return to a normal life, settling down to farm for a while. But he and his rifle, Killdevil, had made too many widows. There was to be no peace in Missouri for him and his family.

He was not a regular member of the Quantrill gang, although Albert Castel, in *Quantrill and his Civil War Guerrillas,* lists him as one of the troops and Carl Breihan, in *Sam Hildebrand, Guerrilla,* uses the introduction to review information from Edward McArtor that his father rode with Quantrill and Hildebrand.

Although the information is attested to by Sam's nephew, L. J. Hildebrand, it is hardly to be trusted as fact. James T. McArtor is on Castel's list of those who rode with Quantrill, and it is possible that he also rode with Hildebrand. However, he reports an event at Kansas City which includes Sam as one of the participants.

In his own book, *The Confessions of Sam Hildebrand,* Sam does not report being in that part of the state. He did, however, make at least one ill-fated raid with Quantrill's men in the Springfield area.

It is known that Sam learned of the guerrillas' Texas haven in Sherman and when the pressure from Pinkerton detectives got too hot in Missouri, Sam took his wife and five children and went there.

While in Texas, his wife Margaret passed away, but a search of the records of Grayson County did not reveal a gravesite. A relative of Sam's, an avid genealogist, states that family tradition says that Margaret died while they were traveling and is buried somewhere along the trail.

Sam returned to Missouri, but he was still a wanted and hunted man, so he moved to Pinkneyville, Illinois.

One day at a bar, Sam thought he was recognized by a customer and went to get his gun. Standing on a crate under a window, he was prepared to shoot the man when a deputy pulled him down and hauled him off to jail.

Sam had several knives hidden on him, and after one had been taken away from him, he sliced open the leg of the deputy with another and the officer shot him in the head.

He was duly buried, but a relative read the story in the St. Louis paper and thought it might be Sam. The body, apparently after being in the grave several days, was exhumed and taken to Farmington, Missouri, and displayed in the courthouse.

Henry Thompson wrote a history of Sam and suggested that the body might not have been Sam's, that perhaps his friends kept quiet so Sam could live in peace and his enemies kept silent so that they could live.

Like Jesse James and Quantrill, Sam was not allowed the luxury of a permanent death. Gene P. Murdock, who did a tremendous amount of research while writing *Sam Hildebrand's Footprints*, claimed that Hildebrand survived the war and lived to an old age. Murdock even includes a picture of Sam as an old man.

Sam's relative also states that the Pinkneyville story does not fit family tradition, which holds that Sam did survive but died of natural causes not long after the war.

Sam's gun, Killdevil, was supposedly placed in the St. Louis Police Department museum, but this writer went there about thirty years ago searching for it, only to be told, "There were some old guns around here, but we don't know what happened to them."

If it is found someday, perhaps hanging over the mantel of a retired police commissioner's fireplace, it will have ninety-two notches in the stock, one for each man Sam killed.

ALLEN PARMER

A relative few of the guerrillas lived a full and successful life. One of these was Allen Parmer, who decided the best place to spend the later years of his life was in Texas with his wife, Susan James, the little sister of Frank and Jesse and a teacher in the Sherman schools.

The *Dallas Morning News,* on Sunday, November 27, 1927, reported in its feature section the death of Allen "Palmer" of Wichita Falls, Texas, a person well known to reporter Fred E. Sutton.

Sutton told of having known "Palmer" over a period of twenty years and having the "pleasure of being thrown with him for a short period."

Once, at the Dallas State Fair, Sutton said he was with "Palmer" and Frank James, where Frank was judging the horse races and "Palmer" was his guest.

The biggest problem with Sutton's story is that he had the subject's name wrong, for the man who died in Wichita Falls in 1927 was Allen H. Parmer, one of Quantrill's bloodiest bushwhackers, husband of Susie James Parmer and the unwanted brother-in-law of Jesse James.

Sutton must have gotten his information from an early biography of Quantrill, for he also spelled "Quantrell" with an "e," which was common in the contemporary books on the guerrilla.

The story is also probably in error about Parmer's exploits at Lawrence, a battle he was likely not even in, since he and the young Jesse James had just joined the raiders. But, as with Jesse, there were those who swore after the war that he was there.

> Allen Palmer [*sic*] and the James boys joined the forces of Quantrill just before the raid on Lawrence and it was here young Palmer made a record of bravery, daring and loyalty to his commander that stayed with him until his last days. These mere boys took the same part in the raid that older men took, and, after they dashed though the town on that memorable day, Palmer was ordered by his chief to retreat and, as he retreated, to burn and kill everything and everybody in sight . . .
> In the midst of this terrible affair, young Palmer was seen

going down the street astride his horse at top speed, a blazing six-shooter in each hand, carrying out to the letter the orders of his chief.

Whether this report came from the fertile mind of the reporter or the age-dimmed memory of Parmer is unknown.

But Parmer was at Centralia, where, according to Sutton, he "distinguished himself," and "where he, with such men as Dave Pool, Frank and Jesse James, Peyton Long and Jim and Cole Younger killed fifty-two men and got away without a scratch."

He fails to mention that most of the men were unarmed. Sutton closed his story by stating that if he should have the privilege of deciding what would be written on Parmer's headstone, it would be: "After, and in spite of all his trials and hardships, here lies a good man."

Some of Parmer's victims and their families might have had a problem accepting that epitaph, for he is listed among those of Quantrill's men who shot down the most people. According to Castel, Peyton Long was the number-one killer, followed by Bill Gower, Allen Parmer, and Dick Maddox.

The family of Lt. G. F. Cunningham, for example, would have rejected the statement that Parmer was a good man. Parmer stuck to Quantrill until the very end in Kentucky, and it was there he met the young Cunningham, who had just completed his time in the Federal service.

When Cunningham, who was only twenty years old, found Parmer about to steal his horse, he grabbed the reins to stop the theft. But Parmer, dressed in a Federal uniform, fired point blank at the young soldier and shot him in the face, killing him. A useless death, for the war was over.

When Quantrill was on his death bed, Parmer was one of the faithful who stood by him and even shed a tear for his fallen leader.

After the death of his chieftain, Parmer, along with Frank James, John Harris, R. M. Venable, Payne Jones, and Andy McGuire, surrendered to Federal authorities on July 26, 1865, and were paroled and permitted to go home.

But home for the raiders would never be the same. The desolation left by Order No. 11 and the antagonistic attitude of the

Union populace made life on the farm very difficult. And after riding for several years with Quantrill, the farm proved to be a very boring place anyway.

Soon, Parmer was riding again, not to defend the downtrodden South but to line his pockets with his share of the loot from bank robberies, which had become a favorite occupation for a number of the guerrillas who had survived.

One such robbery resulted in the issuance of a warrant for Parmer's arrest, along with several others of the old gang, but Parmer was living and working in St. Louis at the time and his employer gave him an alibi for the time of the holdup.

In 1870 Parmer married the strong-willed Susan James, over the strenuous objections of her brother Jesse. According to Breihan, Jesse was so distraught over the wedding that he took morphine in an attempted suicide, but after Parmer moved his bride to Sherman, Jesse and Frank both visited the couple.

The James brothers' baby sister was born in 1849 in Kearney, Missouri, and was named Susan Lavenna James. She taught school in Sherman before marrying Parmer and died March 3, 1889, in Wichita Falls.

Allen and Susie's children included Robert, Flora, Zelma, Allen Jr., who was born in 1882 and died in 1885, Susan Kate, and Feta, who was born in 1887 and lived to a very old age, passing away in 1978.

After finding success in the cattle business in Grayson County, Parmer moved his family to Wichita Falls in 1873 and built a home on Gilbert Creek. In 1905 he became a railroad construction contractor and in 1920 moved to Alpine, Texas.

At the time of his death, there were six other surviving Quantrill bushwhackers, and three of them lived in Texas, which had become a haven for many of the guerrillas after the war.

But perhaps it was his life in Texas for which the former bandit and killer should be remembered, for Sutton had nothing but flowery words for the retired guerrilla:

> His memory was remarkable and he was entertaining indeed as he recited a few of the happenings of his early life with that extreme modesty for which he was noted until the day of his death. It would take a person with a very strong imagination to

ALLEN PALMER MET BEAUTIFUL LITTLE SUSIE JAMES.

A drawing that appeared in the Dallas Morning News *in 1927 when one of the last of Quantrill's men, Allen Parmer (the reporter misspelled his name), passed away in Wichita Falls, Texas. Parmer had married Frank and Jesse James' little sister Susie over the objections of Jesse. Susie was a schoolteacher in Sherman for a time.* —Reprinted with permission of the *Dallas Morning News*

picture this man in his youth as one of the most wonderful horsemen in America, one of the most deadly shots with a six-shooter in either hand, a good soldier, who knew nothing of war except to obey the orders of his commander. And then to picture him in his latter life, in his home, surrounded by his loved one and his friends, who were composed of all the people that knew him as the genial, kindly, courtly Southern gentleman that he was to the day of his death.

Surely the family of Lieutenant Cunningham would have been comforted by the words of the reporter.

FRANK JAMES

At Centralia, another guerrilla, riding next to Frank, was shot and his blood and brains got on his boots. Frank, in his later years, spoofed the idea that the marauders rode with the reins of their horse between their teeth so they could fire two pistols. He would also deny even being at Centralia, since public opinion was very strong in its opposition to the atrocities committed there.

Although not mentioned with those who committed atrocities on their victims, Frank exhibited a complete lack of concern for taking life and certainly did his share of killing innocents.

Frank rode first with Quantrill, then with Anderson, and as it became apparent that the cause was lost and the end of the war was near, he rode to Kentucky with Quantrill instead of heading to Texas with his little brother and others.

It was in Kentucky, after Quantrill had been shot, that Frank surrendered and took the oath, but as with most of the brush fighters, he found no peace when he returned to Missouri. He joined brother Jesse and the Younger brothers in the train and bank robbing business for which they were to become famous, or infamous.

After the fiasco at Northfield, Minnesota, Frank went into hiding and on October 5, 1882, surrendered to Missouri governor Crittenden. He faced two trials for his crimes and was acquitted at both due to lack of evidence.

He had married Annie Ralston in Tennessee in 1874, and they had one child, Robert Franklin.

Texas was certainly included in his travels, since his sister Susie and her husband lived there.

Frank spent the last years of his life making, or trying to make, an income off of his bandit-days fame, joining at one time with Cole Younger in the "Cole Younger and Frank James Historical Wild West Show."

He also worked as a shoe salesman in Paris, Texas, and as a clerk at Sanger-Harris Department Store in Dallas.

When all else failed, he returned to the old homestead in Clay County and charged folks fifty cents each for a tour of the house.

He died on February 18, 1915.

ARCHIE CLEMENTS

Clements survived the war, and along with Dave Poole and other guerrillas, he continued a reign of terror. There probably would have been no peace for the raiders even if they had wanted it, for they had made too many widows, and now most of them, including Archie, had a price on their head.

Archie, perhaps the most sadistic of all the killers, was back in Missouri in the spring of 1865. Although the war was officially over, he continued to believe the "cause" was still alive and told everyone he did not believe that Lee had surrendered.

Clements sent a demand to the commander of the garrison at Lexington to surrender or face the wrath of the bushwhackers:

SIX MILES OUT THE FIELD, May 11, 1865
Major Davis, Lexington, Mo.
    SIR: This is to notify you that I will give you until Friday morning, May 12, 1865, to surrender the town of Lexington. If you surrender we will treat you and all taken as prisoners of war. If we have to take it by storm we will burn the town and kill the soldiers. We have the force, and are determined to have it.
    I am, sir, your obedient servant. A Clements

Major Davis, with 180 men in his garrison, ignored the note, and Archie never did attack Lexington.

Clements' involvement in the Centralia massacre illustrates the depths of evil and sadism to which the guerrillas had sunk. He was with Anderson that September day in 1864, and it was Archie who was given the privilege of being in command of the murder of the innocents as he carried out the order of his chieftain to "parole them."

At Archie's command, the guerrillas opened fire on the unarmed and unclothed soldiers.

Clements went to Lafayette County in the summer of 1866 and visited Poole in Lexington often.

In order to stem the continuing violence on the border counties of Missouri, the governor made a decree that all eligible men should register for the militia.

Surprisingly, Clements, along with Poole and twenty-five

guerrillas, rode into town on December 13 for the expressed purpose of joining the militia. They were all armed to the teeth, and the commander of the garrison ordered them out of town.

Clements and one other man, however, returned to the saloon, and when the soldiers entered to arrest Archie, he fired several shots and ran out the back door, leaped on his horse, and fled down the street.

But his presence in town had brought out more than the three soldiers sent to make the arrest at the City Hotel saloon. As he rode past the courthouse, riflemen stationed inside opened fire, and Clements fell dead in the dust of Franklin Street, his body riddled with bullets.

In a letter to the *Kansas City Times* on August 18, 1876, Jesse James blamed Clements' death on Maj. Bacon Montgomery, the garrison commander who had obviously set a trap to eliminate Clements once and for all: "My opinion is that Bacon Montgomery, the scoundrel who murdered Capt. A. J. Clements, December 13, 1866, is the instigator of all this Missouri Pacific affair."

Like that of his master, Bill Anderson, Archie's body was displayed publicly and pictures were taken. The citizens of Lafayette County sighed in relief.

FLETCHER TAYLOR

After the split with Quantrill in early 1864, Fletcher returned to Missouri and rode with several other bushwhackers, including one Coon Thornton.

On July 10, 1864, Fletcher made a speech condemning unionists.

Fletcher exhibited an ability to express himself, both in spoken and written word, for on July 8, 1864, the *Liberty Tribune* in Jackson County received a letter from "Fletcher P. Taylor, Captain Commanding the County."

He rode with Anderson for a time, but Bloody Bill got a little too bloody for Fletcher when they shot a woman, cut off a male victim's head, began shooting horses for the sport of it, and mutilated bodies at Centralia. Taylor decided to ride his own way.

After leaving Anderson, Fletcher joined forces with John Thrailkill, and on August 8, in a battle with some militiamen near Independence, he received a shotgun wound to his right arm.

The doctor who amputated Fletcher's arm was arrested by the Federals for abetting the outlaws, assuming that the good doctor had operated under his own free will. But the truth was that the bushwhackers had kidnapped him and forced him to perform the surgery. Fortunately for him, he had the foresight to notify a Union officer of the events and was released.

And so, when the guerrillas gathered for the final battle, to pave the way for Gen. Sterling Price's invasion of Missouri in 1864, Fletcher was not there, although even Quantrill had left the lovely Kate to join the battle, which of course did little to advance the cause of Price but lined the bandit's pockets with more loot.

Fletcher survived the war, except for his arm. He resisted the urge to go to Mexico with Jo Shelby and returned to Joplin, where he became vice president and general superintendent of the Joplin Mining and Smelting Company.

His hatred for Quantrill never abated, however, and he relished every opportunity to tell the populace that Kate (Clarke) King had taken the money her lover had left her and opened a whorehouse in St. Louis, a charge repudiated by Leslie in *The Devil Knows How to Ride*.

In his *Roster of Guerrillas,* Carl Breiham states that Fletcher later served as a member of the Missouri legislature.

DAVID POOL(E)

After returning to Missouri from Texas in 1864, Poole rode with Little Archie Clements, his partner is the desecration of dead bodies at Centralia, for a time and then, on May 21, rode into Lexington with eighty-five of his men and surrendered to Colonel Harding. His men laid down their arms and took the oath, and Harding declared, "Bushwhacking has stopped."

But Poole took surrender a step further. He joined with Federal officers in going into the brush and convincing others to come in and take the oath of allegiance. David even revealed many of the bushwhackers' secrets to the Feds.

On March 29, 1865, it was announced in the *Kansas City Journal* that Col. Chester Harding was going to exterminate the guerrillas who were terrorizing the Central District he commanded.

Poole decided to join him, or at least help bring in his old buddies peaceably, as reported in the Official Records of the War of the Rebellion, Series 1, Volume 48, Part 2, pages 705-706:

> . . . Over 200 bushwhackers have accepted the terms offered them at Lexington. Small parties have come here and at other places. The citizens who do not help us are vexed at the course pursued. They think we should meet these fellows in the brush and kill them, or else violate our plighted faith when they are in our power. We have been very anxious to find them in the brush. No one can judge of the difficulties attending the attempt until he tries to do so. It took Dave Pool nearly a week to collect his small band of forty. The men were lying by two and threes in the brush from the Sni Hills to the mouth of the La Mine. It is the same with other gangs; they live with their friend in the country, and are plowing or planting as we pass by. Pool has been out with Lieutenant Saltzman, acting assistant adjutant general, and has showed him some of the tricks of the bushwhackers, among others is that of spreading their blankets across the road and marching their horses on the blankets to prevent a trail being made. Pool is doing good work.[2]

Poole settled down in Lexington, only to be visited on occasion by his old friend Clements, who was an outlaw with a price on his head.

And when some of the old boys robbed the bank in Lexington, the posse that chased them included David Poole and his brother John! However, the newspaper reported that the chase lacked enthusiasm.

Life in Missouri could never be the same for the guerrillas, though, and according to Breihan, Poole moved to the old winter stomping grounds in Sherman, Texas.

GEORGE TODD

At Centralia, Todd, who was known for not having a sense of humor, objected to Poole jumping on the bodies of dead Federal soldiers to count them, protesting that it was inhumane.

After Centralia, Todd continued his reign of terror, riding with Thrailkill on occasion, always leaving a trail of death in his path.

On October 11, 1864, Todd reunited with his old guerrilla buddies as they met with Gen. Sterling Price at Boonville. Price's invasion had already failed when he was turned from his objective of St. Louis at the Battle of Pilot Knob.

Of course, the fact that the guerrillas, who were supposed to be his advance guard, were out killing noncombatants and lining their pockets with loot did not help his cause.

Whether or not Price sanctioned, condoned, or merely tolerated the bushwhackers has been debated since the war. But at Boonville, in dire straits, he was glad to get any help he could.

Orders were given for the rebel guerrillas to go in advance of the army, destroying bridges and railroads, but as soon as they were out of sight of the general, they reverted to their bushwhacker ways. Todd and his men were assigned to Gen. Jo Shelby and stayed close but refused to become a part of the regular army.

On October 21, Shelby met General Blunt and the Kansas Militia just outside of Independence and pushed them back into the city. Todd and his men followed closely.

Perhaps too closely. Just northeast of town, Todd mounted a small hill and raised up in his stirrups to watch the enemy.

A ball struck him in the neck and he suffocated in his own blood. His men carried him into Independence to the home of a Mrs. Burns, where he lived for about an hour. That night his men buried him in the local cemetery and Missourians could rest a little easier knowing that another of the mad killers was gone.

COLE YOUNGER

Cole was one of the first to leave Quantrill, although it is not known when. He never really belonged, anyway, for he really was from one of the fine Missouri families and was never blood-thirsty and cruel like so many of the raiders, except for the time he lined some Federal prisoners up and fired his new Enfield rifle through them to see how many he could kill with one bullet.

The killing of his father and the death of his cousin in the jail collapse had given him a desire for revenge, but he was not in it for the glory or the loot.

From Texas, Younger went to California but returned to Missouri in time to join Jesse and Frank in the bank and train robbery business, although he would later write letters to the newspapers with an alibi for just about every robbery he was accused of being a part of.

A letter written by Cole to his brother-in-law, Lycurgus Jones, appeared in the *Missouri Review,* published in Pleasant Hill, Missouri:

> Dear Curg:
>   You may use this letter in your own way. I will give you the outline and sketch of whereabouts and actions at the time certain robberies with which I am charged. At the time of certain bank robberies, I was gathering cattle in Ellis County, Texas, cattle that I bought from Pleas Taylor and Rector. This can be proven by both of them, also by Sheriff Barkley and fifty other respectable men of that county.

The ill-fated bank robbery in Northfield, Minnesota, led to the downfall of the James–Younger gang and the friendship of Cole and Jesse.

All three Younger brothers, Jim, Bob, and Cole, were badly wounded when the alarm was sounded and the townspeople rallied to drive off the eight robbers, killing two. Only Jesse and Frank escaped without injury.

Jim Younger was so badly wounded it was thought he was not

going to make it, and Jesse suggested to Cole that they go ahead and kill him, as he was slowing down their escape.

"Damn you, Jesse James," hissed Cole, "you are indeed a cold-hearted devil. If any or all of you have such an idea, go take your own paths, and I hope we never meet again. To kill my own brother! I'll stay with him and fight until the very end, and then carry him on my shoulders until I, myself, fall."[3]

That was the end of the relationship between Cole and Jesse, but Frank would remain a friend of Cole's, even appearing in his Wild West show.

The Younger brothers were captured and sentenced to prison for life. Jim had been shot five times; one shot shattered his upper jaw and lodged near his brain. During his years in prison, he endured much pain.

Bob Younger suffered from tuberculosis and after thirteen years in prison died in the state penitentiary at Stillwater. He had been a model prisoner.

In July of 1901, Jim and Cole were released from prison, and on October 19, 1902, Jim killed himself at the Reardon Hotel in St. Paul, either because the parole board refused to allow him to marry or because the young lady he loved refused him.

Cole became a prolific writer of letters. Some were written to a professional writer, J. W. Buel, and for the most part were meant to convince the world that the bushwhackers were really not all that bad.

He also shed some light on the military status of the guerrillas, although it contradicts some other reports. In a letter to J. A. Dacus, Cole wrote:

> The idea had gotten abroad that the guerrillas of Missouri were not recognized by the Confederates and Confederate soldiers. That is false. They took the same oath that was administered to all Confederate soldiers, and were recognized by all the generals in the Trans-Mississippi Department. The Confederate War Department refused to give Quantrill a commission as Colonel of partisan rangers independent of the generals command of the different departments west of the Mississippi; but they recognized him as captain with authority to recruit as many companies for the Confederate States as he

could. Now as for myself, I took the same oath and it was ad-
ministered by the same officers that swore all of Col. Up Hays
men in. Quantrill and all of his men took the same oath. I was
personally recognized by nearly all the generals in the Trans-
Mississippi Department-as a guerrilla, it is true, but as an officer of the Confederate army at the same time.[4]

Younger also claimed that he drew pay as a Confederate officer from August 1862 until he left the service to go to
California.

Cole lived a fruitful life after prison, with frequent visits to
Texas with his Wild West show.

He passed away on March 21, 1916, and was buried next to
his brothers.

WILLIAM GREGG

Bill Gregg returned to Jackson County, and he and his wife,
Lizzie, had ten children, but tragedy was to stalk the ex-
guerrilla. A son died as an infant, and on the same day, their
fifteen-year-old twin daughters died of typhoid.

Bill had a hard time holding a job and worked as a handy-
man and even as a deputy sheriff. He suffered from rheumatism
and died of "senile atrophy of the heart," on April 22, 1916. He
also had cancer. Ten days later, Lizzie, his wife of fifty-one years,
followed him in death.

His greatest claim to postwar fame came when he wrote, at
the urging of William Connelley, his own record of the raiders'
adventures, entitled *A Little Dab of History without Embellishment*.

He had been giving information to Connelley, not realizing
the northerner was writing a history of the raiders that showed
them as something less than Confederate heroes.

Perhaps his greatest shock was when Quantrill's mother
came to visit and Gregg learned that there was no "older
brother" and that Quantrill's story was all a fabrication.

JOHN THRAILKILL

On September 14, 1864, two weeks before Price's battle at Pilot Knob, Thrailkill joined forces with Todd and rode into Keytesville early in the morning. Thrailkill rode up under a white flag and demanded that the thirty-five-man garrison surrender or be killed, and Lt. Anthony Pleyer, on the advice of the Carroll County sheriff, promptly capitulated.

Seven of the Paw Paw's[5] joined the bushwhackers, and Thrailkill paroled the rest, signing the paroles Major, Commanding Recruits.

He introduced Lieutenant Pleyer to Todd, and the young officer realized how fortunate he was when Todd told him, "I'm the bushwhacker Todd. You need not consider me a Confederate officer."

After ravaging the town, burning the courthouse, and killing a prominent unionist, Todd and Thrailkill headed for Howard Country, but not before Thrailkill made a speech on the virtues of the Confederacy.[6]

Thrailkill was riding with Fletch Taylor when he was shot and then took part in the Centralia debacle. Some claimed that Todd and Thrailkill actually directed the Centralia massacre.

But his greatest talent, perhaps, was in recruiting for the Confederacy, and it was on this mission in July of 1863 that he told some strangers he was recruiting for the regular service, even refusing to talk to one of them who said he wanted to join the bushwhacking department.

"I don't wish you to join me. There are two arms of the service to which I am opposed, one is bushwhacking and the other is Jayhawking."

He advised them to find a Confederate officer and join the regular forces, but the men turned out to be Union spies and arrested Thrailkill, fortunately for him, as a recruiter for the Confederate Army. He was sentenced to prison for the duration of the war.

At the close of the war, Thrailkill went to Mexico with Jo Shelby.

He seemed to be a warrior who wavered between the regular

war and the guerrilla methods. His contributions to the bush-whackers, however, did not even justify a mention of his name in John Connelley's book.

QUANTRILL

Quantrill returned to Missouri in the spring of 1864 but abandoned his bushwhacker role and went into seclusion with his mistress, Kate Clarke, coming out to help in the final invasion of Missouri by Price. In December, along with thirty-three still-loyal comrades, he rode to Kentucky.

Some historians have implied that Quantrill was on his way to Washington to assassinate President Lincoln but cancelled the trip when he learned that John Wilkes Booth had accomplished the task for him. However, there is no physical evidence to prove this.

Camped out in Spencer County, the little band was discovered and attacked by troops under Capt. Edward Terrell, and in the effort to escape, Quantrill was shot in the back, the bullet veering downward and striking his spine.

Captain Terrell carried his prize, who was in pitiful pain, to the military hospital in Louisville, where he made a full confession of his sins and embraced the Catholic faith before his death.

He died on June 6, 1865, and was buried in Louisville, but his mother had his bones exhumed and moved back to Ohio. Some of the bones did not make it home, though, for they were sold by the man his mother had paid to carry out the reburial.

An old friend of the family, W. W. Scott, not only figured out a way to turn a fast dollar with the Quantrill bones but served as a primary source for William Connelley in his *Quantrill and the Border Wars*.

Recently, in Potosi, Missouri, a young lady told me she was related to Quantrill but sometime after the war, the family name was changed to Cantrell. It speaks poorly of your contribution to society when your ancestors don't want anyone to know of your kinship.

KATE (KING) CLARKE

The story that Kate King Clarke, after receiving Quantrill's belongings after his death in Kentucky, used them to open a house of prostitution in St. Louis is questionable. The story was told by Fletch Taylor, and considering the hard feelings between Quantrill and Taylor after their falling-out in Texas, his testimony is certainly to be questioned.

Leslie, in *The Devil Knows How to Ride,* completely refutes Taylor's claim, stating that Kate opened a boarding house in St. Louis and married a wealthy man, J. R. Claiborne.[7]

According to Leslie, she married three more times, the last being to one of the "inmates" at the Jackson County Home for the Aged, known in those days as "the poor farm."

She passed away on January 9, 1930, at the age of eighty-two, and after a delay of a month while relatives were found to pay for the funeral, she was buried in the Maple Hill Cemetery, Kansas City, Kansas.

She remained a mystery woman, insisting to the end that Quantrill was the only man she ever loved and that he was not the personification of evil that he had been made out to be.

JAMES BLUNT

Blunt was relieved of his command after Baxter Springs. After a short time as a recruiter, he was reinstated as a battlefield general when Sterling Price made his last-ditch invasion of Missouri in the fall of 1864, and he took part in more than twenty of the little battles that drove Price from the state.

After the war, Blunt resumed his medical practice in Leavenworth and then moved to Washington, D.C. In his later years, he became disturbed and was confined to a mental asylum before his death on July 27, 1881.

GENERAL E. KIRBY SMITH

After Lee's surrender at Appomattox Court House on April 9, 1865, Lt. Gen. E. Kirby Smith remained the last holdout of the Confederate army, commanding the Trans-Mississippi Department. Early in May, there were no Confederate units operating east of the Mississippi.

At Marshall, the capital of Confederate Missouri, in exile, the governors of Arkansas, Louisiana, and Missouri, along with a representative from Texas, met on May 14, 1865, with Smith and advised him to surrender. Jo Shelby, however, threatened to arrest Smith unless he continued to fight.

When the Federals tried to negotiate Smith's surrender, his terms were so outrageous they were refused, and he threatened to invade west Texas.

Smith still wanted to hold on, but the news of Lee's surrender gave the soldiers in his command an excuse to leave for home and the army simply disintegrated.

As late as May 18, Smith rode a stagecoach to Houston in an effort to rally his troops. He finally surrendered to Brig. Gen. E.R.S. Canby on May 26, 1865.

Smith, along with perhaps as many as 2,000 men, headed into Old Mexico. Dressed in civilian clothes which included a calico shirt and a silk scarf, he rode a mule across the Rio Grande.

After the war, he served as president of the University of Nashville and taught at the University of the South at Sewanee, Tennessee. He passed away on March 28, 1893.

THOMAS EWING

Outside of Order No. 11, Ewing is best remembered for his stand at Pilot Knob, where less than a thousand Federal troops in the hole in the ground called Fort Davidson stopped Sterling Price's invasion force in its tracks, probably saving St. Louis from capture. Oddly enough, he almost missed the battle, as he had started home to Ohio as his wife was giving birth.

After the war, he worked as a lawyer once again. Some historians have claimed that his political career was doomed because of Order No. 11, but probably what happened in Missouri during the war had very little affect on elections in Ohio.

He moved to Washington, where he turned down appointments to U.S. Attorney General and Secretary of War. As a lawyer, he defended three of the Lincoln assassination conspirators, Samuel Arnold, Edward Spangler, and the doctor who tended Booth's leg, Samuel Mudd.

He did serve in the House of Representatives for two terms. He ran for governor in 1879, but George Caleb Bingham, who had painted the famous depiction of the result of Order No. 11, mounted a campaign against Ewing and he was defeated by just over 17,000 votes. How much influence Bingham, who passed away before the election, had on voters is not known.

On January 20, 1896, Ewing was crossing a busy street in downtown Yonkers when he was struck by a cable car and killed.

GENERAL HENRY MCCULLOCH

Perhaps the Confederate officer who suffered the most anguish because of the guerrillas, Henry McCulloch would go down in history as the "brother of Ben McCulloch, who was killed at Pea Ridge."

Henry had numerous disagreements with Gen. Sterling Price, most of them about who held the highest rank early in the war. He saw very little real conflict, but as director of the District of northeast Texas he had all the headaches he could handle, from disobedient guerrillas to the thousands of deserters hiding out in Jernigan Thicket, to Gen. Kirby Smith over in Shreveport.

After the war, he settled back into farming in Guadalupe County and for a time served as the superintendent of the Texas Deaf and Dumb Asylum. He died at Rockport on March 12, 1895.

STERLING PRICE

Perhaps Sterling Price's greatest blunder was at Pilot Knob, Missouri, where an ill-advised charge, led by Gen. W. L. Cabell, against Thomas Ewing's small band cost him a thousand troops in one charge at the earthen Fort Davidson. More importantly, the charge delayed his potential march on St. Louis long enough for reinforcements to arrive to protect the city.

His army, turned away from its primary target, swung west across central Missouri and fought skirmishes all the way until Westport, where he was defeated and the retreat to Arkansas began. The last-ditch invasion was doomed from the beginning, for most of Price's army were untrained recruits, some very young and some very old, and many of them were without weapons or even shoes.

In his lengthy report on his "Missouri Expedition," written on December 28, 1864, and addressed to Brig. Gen. W. R. Boggs, chief of staff at Shreveport, Price only mentioned the guerrillas once:

> Captain Anderson, who reported to me that day with company of about 100 men, was immediately sent to destroy the North Missouri Railroad. At the same time Quantrill was sent with the men under his command to destroy the Hannibal and Saint Joseph Railroad, to prevent the enemy, if possible, from throwing their forces in my front from Saint Louis. These officers I was informed afterward did effect some damage to the roads, but none of any material advantage, and totally failed in the main object proposed, which was to destroy the large railroad bridge that was in the end of St. Charles County.

Sterling Price learned too late what Henry McCulloch had already found out the hard way: you could not depend on the guerrillas to carry out a military operation.

He was called before a board of inquiry in April of 1865 in Shreveport to answer for the bungled invasion and heard his officers report on the lack of discipline and hesitancy in decision-making.

At one point, a witness was asked, "Do you know of General Price sending a detachment from Boonville to destroy the Perraque Bridge, on the North Missouri Railroad; and if so, to whom were the orders given? Give the names and character."

The informant answered, "They were given to Colonels Anderson and Quantrill. They were the most distinguished partisan leaders, and were the terror of the enemy in that section and accustomed to operating on railroads."

Of course, Price's orders to Anderson had been found on his body.

Price went to Mexico after the war, knowing that with the Federals in control and slavery a thing of the past, his potential as a tobacco farmer or as a politician was at a low ebb.

He returned to his beloved state in 1867, broke and in poor health, and passed away in St. Louis eight months later.

Historians have argued whether or not Price, a stately gentleman of the Old South tradition, approved of the guerrilla warfare. It is interesting that in his communiqués he referred to Anderson as "Captain," giving some credence to the claim that the bushwhackers were legitimate Confederate soldiers.

The probability is that he did not approve of their methods of combat or recognize them as regular army (based on communiques about Quantrill and other guerrilla leaders). But as he faced the hopeless reality of the impossible odds of the South winning, he was grasping at straws to find a way to defeat the Union forces.

To this end, it would appear that he overlooked the methods of operation used by the guerrillas, as opposed to "civilized warfare." During his last great gasp, the invasion in the fall of 1864, he requested the bushwhackers to serve as an advance guard, destroying railways and communications. The guerrillas, however, at this stage of the war, had forgotten the "cause"—if they had ever really embraced it—and spent the final months of the war lining their pockets with loot and killing personal enemies and innocent citizens.

JAMES BOURLAND

Bourland, a Texas patriot, once again proved his value to the state by defending it against an Indian attack at Fort Belknap in October of 1864.

In spite of his service to the Republic of Texas, which began as early as 1841 when he led a volunteer company against Indians, his service during the Mexican War as a member of the Texas Mounted Rifles under William C. Young, his election to the Senate of the First and Second state legislatures, and his exemplary service in the district during the Civil War, Bourland lived with the stigma of being known as "the hangman of Texas."

Hounded by the memory of the multiple hangings at Gainesville and the reports of his hash treatment of prisoners and even his own men, after the war Bourland was acquitted of any wrongdoing by a civil court and lived in seclusion, passing away on August 20, 1879.

SOPHIA BUTT PORTER

Sophia gained the title of "the Confederate Paul Revere" when she opened up her wine cellar to a troop of Federal soldiers while she rode to warn James Bourland that they were looking for him.

Whether fact or legend, the story never made the official records of the War of the Rebellion, but eyewitnesses backed up her story.

Soon after Bourland had stopped at Glen Eden on his way to Fort Washita on the other side of the Red River, Yankee soldiers came looking for him.

Sophia, so the story goes, opened up her ample wine cellar after preparing a meal for the Federals. When they were drunk, she locked them in and rode a mule across the partially frozen river.

It is unlikely that she rode all the way to Fort Washita, but Bourland was warned and the story became accepted. Sophia, it must be remembered, had a way of enhancing stories, and there are parts of this one that are questionable.

Later she took her money (gold, not Confederate paper, for in spite of her faults, Sophia was no fool) and went to Waco with a few of her servants. There she met the man who was to be her fourth husband, James Porter. Porter had served the Confederacy in a Missouri cavalry regiment and, seeing the war was lost, had headed for Mexico. On the way, he met Sophia and headed back north to Glen Eden.

In 1869 she was gloriously converted to Christianity at a Methodist brush arbor meeting, conducted by Reverend Jacob Monroe Binkley.

Sophia, dressed in an orange satin dress, threw herself at the pastor's feet, who declared "the sun, the moon, and the stars were all against her becoming a Christian." He further questioned her remarkable conversion by not allowing her to become a member of the church for twelve years because of her past life.[8] Apparently the good Reverend Binkley, who had begun his career as a lecturer on temperance,[9] had heard about the parties at Glen Eden.

However, two papers found in the Sherman Public Library, one written by a family member, state that she joined the church in 1869 and was received by Reverend Binkley, who was by her bedside when she died.

With her new found religion, the dances at Glen Eden came to a halt and Sophia spent the rest of her life supporting the church.

During the 1870s, James and Sophia built Glen Eden into an empire of cotton and cattle. Porter died on September 10, 1886, and Sophia was once more a widow.

Sophia Suttenfield Aughinbaugh Coffee Butt Porter died on August 27, 1897, at the age of eighty-one. Her estate was valued at $18,087.17. Personal property included 14 cows, 46 hogs, mules, horses, a carriage, a sewing machine, a tent and wagon sheet, furniture, five stands of bees, 25 gallons of wine, 120 pounds of ham, and 143 head of poultry.[10]

APPENDIX I

List of those who rode with Quantrill

Agen, (name not known)
Akers, Slyvester
Anderson, James (Jim)
Anderson, William
Archie, Hugh
Archie, William
Asbury, A. E.
Atchison, Bes
Baker, Sgt. John
Baker, Valentine
Barbie, Johnson
Barker, John
Barnhill, John
Bassham, Ike
Basham, Solomon
Basham, William
Beard, Frank
Beard, William
Bell, Thomas
Beit, Mort
Berry, Ike
Berry, Richard
Bishop, Jack (John)
Bisset, James
Black, (name not known)
Blackmore, William
Bledsoe, William

Blunt, Andrew (Andy)
Blythe, John
Blythe, Theodore
Bochman, Charley
Bowles, Jeptha
Brady, (name not known)
Brandy, Mass
Brinker, John
Brookins, Henry
Brooks, Samuel
Broomfield, Benjamin
Brown, Harvey/John
Buford, Henry
Bunch, Oliver
Burns, Richard
Burton, Peter
Campbell, Andrew
Campbell, Doc
Carlyle, (name not known)
Carr, Nathan
Carr, William
Carter, Harrison
Carroll, Dolf
Castle, Theodore
Chatman, John
Chambers, Burney
Chiles, Jim Crow

171

Chiles, Joel
Chiles, Kit
Chiles, Richard
Chiles, William
Clark, Marcellus
Clarke, Sam C.
Clayton, George
Clayton, James
Clement, Archie
Clement, Henry
Clifton, Sam
Commons, Smith
Constable, Sam
Corley, Dock
Corum, Alfred
Corum, James
Corum, John
Coward, Henry
Crabtree, Riley
Creek, Abner
Creek, Creth
Creek, Sid
Creek, Pate
Cummins, Jim
Candhill, (name not known)
Cunningham, Albert
Daily, George
Dalton, J. Frank
Dancer, Jim
Davinport, William
Davis, Jo
Debenhorst, Paul
Dehart, E. P.
Devers, Alva
Deavers, Arthur
Devers, James
Dickerson, John B.
Dobson, James
Edmundson, J. F.
Ellington, Richard
Emery, Jeff
Evers, J. C.

Esters, Joshua
Estes, (name not known)
Evans, James
Evans, Tom
Farley, Peter
Farrets, John
Fickell, Joseph
Finnigan, Samuel
Fisher, John
Flannery, Ike
Flannery, John
Flannery, Si
Flournoy, John
Fox, (name not known)
Freeman, Will
Frisby, John
Fristoe, William
Fry, Frank
Fugitt, Press
Fulton, Thomas
Garrett, (name not known)
Gatey, Sam
Gaw, William
George, Dave
George, Gabriel
George, Hicks
George, Hiram
Gibson, James
Gilcrhist, Joseph
Glasscock, Richard
Goodman, Thomas M.
Gordon, Silas
Graham, Jack
Gray, Frank
Greenwood, William
Gregg, Frank J.
Gregg, William
Grindstaff, William
Groomer, Garrett
Grosvenor, (name not known)
Guess, Hiram
Haick, (name not known)

Hale, Doc
Hall, George
Hall, Isaac
Hall, Joseph
Hall, Robert (Bob)
Hall, Thomas
Hallar/Haller, Abe
Haller, William
Halley, (name not known)
Halloran, Will
Hamilton, Tom
Hamet/Hamlett, Jesse
Hampton, John
Harbaugh, Frank
Hardin, Joseph
Harris, John
Harris, Rueben
Harris, Thomas
Harrison, Ki
Hart, Joe
Hays, John (William)
Hays, Perry
Hays/Hayes, Upton
Hegen, Edward
Helms, Polk
Helton, David
Hensburg, William
Hendricks, James
Henry, Thomas
Higbee, Charles
Hildebrand, Sam
Hill, Thomas
Hill, Tucker
Hills, Woot (Wood)
Hilton, Dave
Hinds, James
Hink, Edward
Hinton, Otho (Otto)
Hockensmith, Clarke
Hockensmith, Henry
Hillings, Washington
Holt, Joseph

Holtzclaw, Clifton
Hope, John
Hotie, Richard
House, John
Hoy, Perry
Hubbard, John
Hudspeth, George
Hudspeth, Robert
Hudspeth, Rufus
Huffaker, Moses
Hughes, John T.
Hulse, William
Hunt, Tom
Jackson, George
Jackson, John
James, Frank
James, Jesse
James, William
Jarrette, John
Jenkins, Snowy
Jessup, Sam
Jobson, Presley
Jobson, Smith
Johnson, Oliver
Johnson, Richard
Johnson, Socrates
Jones, Jim
Jones, Payne
Kelly, James
Kelly, Tom
Kennedy, David
Kennedy, Sterling
Kenny, Dick
Kerr, Nathan
Ketchum, Al
Key, Foster
King, Silas
Kinney, Richard
Knight, (name not known)
Koger, Edward
Koger, John
Langdon, George

Larett, John
Lea, Joe
Lee, Albert
Lee, Joseph
Lester, Frank
Letten, Ling
Lewis, Bart
Liddel, James Andrew
Lilly, James
Lisle, Marston
Litten, Ling
Little, James
Little, John
Little, Thomas
Long, Peyton
Lotspeach, William
Luckett, (name not known)
Maddox, George
Maddox, Morgan
Maddox, Richard
Magruder, Rezin
Majors, Newt
Marshall, Edward
Marshall, James
Martinez, Leon
Masterson, Hiram
Mattox, M. T.
Maupin, Thomas
Maxwell, Ambrose
Maxwell, Thomas
McAninch, Henry
McArtor, James T.
McCabe, James
McBurgis, (name not known)
McCorkle, James (Job)
McCorkle, John
McCorkle, Joseph
McCorkle Joshua
McCorkle, Thomas
McCoy, Arthur
McCoy, Richard
McDowell, John

McGuire, Andy
McQuire, William
McIlvaine, John
McIver, John
McMurtry, Lee
McMurtry, (name not known)
Mead, Jacob (John)
Miller, Clell
Miller, Edward
Monkers, Red
Moody, Jasper
Morris, James
Morrow, Benjamin J.
Morrow, George
Morton, Wade
Murray, Plunk
Nagle, Patrick
Ney, Foss
Nicholson, Arch
Nicholson, Joseph
Noland, Edward
Noland, Henry
Noland, John
Noland, William
Norfolk, John
O'Donnell, Pat
Ogden, Henry
Oliphant, Newton
Owens, Thomas
Palmer, Chris
Parmer, Allen
Parker, Will
Parr, Buster
Parr, Mik
Parvin (Priven), Hence
Parvin (Priven), Lafe
Patteron, Henry
Pence, Bud
Pence, A. D. "Donnie"
Perkins, (name not known)
Perry, Joab
Peyton, (name not known)

Phillips, Edward
Pool(e), David
Pool, John
Pope, Sam
Porter, Henry
Potts, Levi
Pringle, John
Quantrill, William
Railly, Lon
Rains, John
Ralston, Crockett
Reed/Read, James
Rennick, Chat (Clarke)
Reynolds, William
Rice, Ten
Ridings, William
Robinson, Dick
Robinson, George
Robinson (Robertson), Gooly
Robinson, William
Roder, William
Rodes, Jasper
Rollen, (name not known)
Ross, John
Rudd, John
Runnels, William
Rupe, John "Dock"
Ryan, Volney
Sanders, Matt
Sanders, Ted
Saunders, Charles
Schull, Boon
Scott, Albert
Scott, Fernando
Shepherd, Frank
Shepherd, George
Shepherd, Martin
Shepherd, Oliver
Simonds/Simmons, (name not known)
Simmons, George
Skaggs, Larkin Melton

Smith, Perry
Smith, William
Smoot, Archibald
Sorrels, Thomas
Southerland, Zack
Southwick, A. B.
Southwick, C. H.
Stevenson, Jim
Stewart, Charles
Stewart, William
Stone, William
Storey, Bud
Strother, William
Stuart, William
Stugeon, (name not known)
Sutherland, Jack
Sutherland, Zeke
Swisby, Oscar
Talcott, Parker
Talley, George
Tarkington, William
Tate, David
Taylor, Fletcher
Thompson, James
Thompson, Oliver
Thrailkill, John
Tigue, Nat
Todd, George
Todd, Robert
Todd, Thomas
Todd, W. C.
Toler (Toller), Bill
Taley/Tooly, J. B.
Tolliver, Anson
Tomlinson, Clarence
Toothman/Toothum, William
Traber, Thomas
Traber, Zach
Trow, Harrison
Tucker, James
Tucker, Morris J.
Tucker, William

Tuckett, Thomas
Turpin, Dick
Vandiver, Louis
Van Meter, John
Vaughan, Dan
Vaughan, Joe
Vaughn, James
Vaughan, Jim
Venable, Randolph
Wade, David
Wade, Newman
Wade, Sam
Walker, Andrew Y.
Ward, Robert
Warren, John Thomas
Wayman, F. Luther
Wayman, Matt
Webb, Charles
Webb, Pres
Webster, John
Webster, Noah
Welby, James
Welch, Warren
Wells, Craid
Wells, Polk
West, Richard
White, James

White, John
Whitsett, James
Wigginton, George
Wigginton, Will
Wilcox, Lawrence
Wilkinson, James
Will, Jack
Williams, Dan
Williams, Henry
William, Jack
Williams, Jim
Wilson, John (Dave)
Winchester, William
Wood, Bennett
Wood, David
Wood, Hop
Wood, Robert
Woodruff, Silas
Woodward, William
Wyatt, Al
Wyatt, Cave
Yager/Yeager, Richard
Young, Joseph
Younger, Coleman
Younger, Jim
Younger, John
Yowell, Bill

Source: Richard A. Ensminger, Quantrill Guerrilla File, University of Kansas State.

APPENDIX II

DEM BONES, DEM BONES GONNA WALK AROUND

Several of the bushwhackers had a hard time staying dead and keeping all of their parts with them. Sam Hildebrand was dug up from his grave in Illnois and displayed at the St. Francois County courthouse in Farmington, Missouri, before finally being reinterred in a cemetery in Elvins, Missouri (now Park Cities).

Bloody Bill Anderson supposedly lost his head, but when he was finally laid to rest, it was buried with him, even though they did get the date of his birth wrong on the tombstone.

Even the great Stonewall Jackson's body was buried in one place and his amputated arm in another cemetary.

But no one's bones had a harder time finding peace and rest than those of William Clarke Quantrill.

On June 7, 1865, *The Louisville Journal* reported: "William Clark, alias Quantrill, captain Fourth Missouri cavalry, who was wounded and captured as a guerrilla near Taylorsville, Ky., May 10, died in a military prison hospital in this city, yesterday evening about 4 o'clock."[1]

The recent convert to Catholic religion may have finally been delivered from whatever torments drove him to murder innocents, but his bones were about to do a lot of walking.

Quantrill's mother sent a family friend, W. W. Scott, to Kentucky to exhume his body and bring it home to Canal Dover.

Canal Dover resisted having such a notorious killer buried in their graveyard but finally relented, and Quantrill's bones were finally laid to rest—except for his skull, three arm bones, and a couple of shin-bones, which Scott kept for himself. He donated the shin bones to the Kansas Historical Society and tried to sell the skull.

However, J. E. Duffy reported that he had met and talked with

177

Quantrill, who was supposedly living at Coal Harbor, Vancouver Island, British Columbia. When the story was reported in the Topeka, Kansas, papers on August 9, 1907, the society took the bones off of display and placed them in storage.

Duffy was murdered shortly after the story in the papers appeared, beaten to death by two visitors from the United States. The reported sighting of Quantrill was only one of many but certainly was the most creditable.

In 1910, the Zeta Chapter of the Alpha Pi fraternity obtained a skull from Scott's son, placed red lights in the eye sockets, and used it in their secret ceremonies. The initiation of a new member involved placing his hand on the skull while taking the oath of loyalty to the fraternity.

The skull stayed in the possession of the society until it disbanded in 1942, and Nelson McMillan, a member, kept it in his basement, displaying it at the 1960 reunion of the organization. In 1972, he donated it to the Dover Historical Society.

Whether or not it is really the skull of William Clarke Quantrill has never been proven . . . or disproven.

Source: *The Devil Knows How to Ride,* Edward E. Leslie.

NOTES

Preface

1. *Reminiscences of the Boys in Gray 1861-1865*, compiled by Mamie Yeary.

2. *Quantrill and the Border Wars*, William Elsey Connelley, Torch Press, 1910.

3. "A Little Dab of History Without Embellishment," William H. Gregg, unpublished document dated October 5, 1906. Western Historical Manuscript Collection, 23 Ellis Library (University of Missouri–Columbia)

4. *Bloody Dawn*, Thomas Goodrich, Kent State University Press, 1991.

5. Official Records of the War of the Rebellion, Series 1, Volume 3, p. 459.

6. *Tainted Breeze, The Great Hanging at Gainesville, Texas, 1862,* Richard B. McCaslin, Louisiana State Universtiy Press, 1994.

Chapter 1

1. *Brush Men and Vigilantes*, David Pickering and Judy Falls, Texas A&M Press, 2000.

2. Official Records of the War of the Rebellion, Series 4, Volume 1, pages 323-325.

3. *Rebel Religion*, E. M. Boswell, *Civil War Times Illustrated*, October 1972.

4. *Texas in 1850*, Melinda Rankin, 1850. Reprinted in 1966 by Texian Press.

5. *The Fremantle Diary, the Journal of Lieutenant Colonel Arthur James Lyon Fremantle*, Little, Brown and Co., 1954.

6. *Austin to Josiah Fell*, February 24, 1820, The Austin Papers.

7. *Millennial Harbinger XIII*, p. 238, Bethany, Virginia.

8. *History of Texas II*, H. Yoakum, pp. 219-227.

9. *Civil War Times III, Rebel Religion*, E. M. Boswell, October 1972.

10. *Grayson County Illustrated History*, Historical Publishing, Landom and Smith, 1967.

11. *Texas in the War,* compiled by Marcus J. Wright, Brig. Gen., C.S.A., edited and noted by Harold B. Simpson, Co., U.S.A.F. (Ret.), Hill Junior College Press, 1965.

12. *Texas on the Road to Secession,* Volume II, Joe T. Timmons, Doctor of Philosophy Dissertation, Chicago, 1973.

13. Ibid.

14. *Brush Men and Vigilantes,* David Pickering and Judy Falls, Texas A&M Press, 2000.

15. *Writings of Thomas Barrett,* Sherman, Texas, Public Library.

Chapter 2

1. *Quantrill and the Border Wars,* William Elsey Connelley, The National Historical Society, 1909.

2. Horizontal beams.

3. Lieutenant Pond received the Congressional Medal of Honor for his action at Fort Blair, thirty-five years after the fact.

4. Connelley disputes this claim, stating that it was impossible. But he failed to recognize the firepower of the guerrilla pistols. *Quantrill and the Border Wars,* John Connelley.

5. Official Records of the War of the Rebellion, Volume 22, Part I, pp. 696-697.

6. Official Records of the War of the Rebellion, Series 1, Part 2, Volume 26, pp. 339-340.

7. Official Records of the War of the Rebellion. Report of Maj. Gen. James G. Blunt, U.S. Army. Headquarters District of the Frontier, Fort Scott, Kansas, October 1863.

Chapter 3

1. Official Records of the War of the Rebellion, Series 1, Volume 8, p. 507.

2. *The Confessions of Sam Hildebrand,* Dr. A. Wendell Keith and James W. Evans, 1870.

3. *Branded as Rebels,* compiled by Joanne Chiles Eakin and Donald R. Hale, 1993. Sherman, Texas, Public Library.

4. *Quantrill and the Border Wars,* William Elsey Connelley, The Torch Press, 1910.

5. Official Records of the War of the Rebellion, Series 1, Volume 22, page 715.

6. Castel says that Henry Coleman was a slaveholder and pro-Southerner who opposed secession. *William Clarke Quantrill, His Life and Times,* Albert Castel, Frederick Fell, 1962.

7. Ibid. Castel states that Walley murdered Henry Coleman because Cole had cut in on him at a dance.

8. Cole was known as "Bud" in those days. Apparently, Loan had misunderstood the nickname.

9. Official Records of the War of the Rebellion, Series 1, Volume 22, Part 2, p. 80.

10. *Inside War,* Michael Fellman, Oxford University Press, 1989.

11. *Quantrill and the Border Wars,* John Elsey Connelley, Torch Press, 1910.

12. Official Records of the War of the Rebellion, Series 1, Volume 8, p. 57.

13. Official Records of the Rebellion, Series I, Volume 8, pp. 514-515.

14. *Tainted Breeze: The Great Hanging at Gainesville, Texas, in 1862.* Richard B. McCaslin.

Chapter 5

1. "Colbert's Ferry." *Chronicles of Oklahoma*, summer 1979, Morris L. Britton.

2. Official Records of the War of the Rebellion, Series 1, Volume 22, Part 1, pp. 700-701.

3. Official Records of the War of the Rebellion, Series 1, Volume 22, Part 1, pp. 700-701.

4. *Quantrill and the Border Wars*, William Elsey Connelley, The Torch Press, 1910.

5. Official Records of the War of the Rebellion, Series 1, Part 2, Volume 22, p. 715.

6. Neville, A. W. *Red River Valley, Then and Now*, North Texas Publishing Company, Paris, Texas, 1948.

7. *Grayson County Illustrated History*, Landom and Smith, Historical Publishers, 1967.

8. Henry Vaden, Lucas Papers, Sherman Public Library.

9. Official Records of the War of the Rebellion, Series 1, Volume 26, Part 2, p. 348.

10. *Brush Men and Vigilantes*, David Pickering and Judy Falls, Texas A&M Press, 2000.

11. Official Records of the War of the Rebellion, Series 1, Volume 34, Part 2, pp. 941-943.

12. Ibid. Series 1, Volume 26, p. 526.

Chapter 6

1. *Mistress of Glen Eden: The Life and Times of Texas Pioneer Sophia Porter*, Sherrie S. McLeRoy, Sherman, Texas.

Chapter 7

1. Lookout Station, Missouri, where the Confederates had attacked a train in 1861.

2. *Sherman Herald-Democrat*, September 12, 1926.

Chapter 8

1. *Quantrill and the Border Wars*, John Elsey Connelley, Torch Press, 1910.
2. Ibid.
3. Ibid

Chapter 9

1. Official Records of the War of the Rebellion, Series 1, Volume 26, part 2, pp. 382-383.
2. Ibid. Series 1, Volume 26, Part 2, pp. 430-431.
3. Ibid.
4. *Mistress of Glen Eden*, Sherrie S. McLeRoy.

Chapter 10

1. *Quantrill and the Border Wars,* John Elsey Connelley, Torch Press, 1910.

2. Official Records of the War of the Rebellion, Series 1, Volume 22, Part 2, Page 1037.

3. W. L. Potter states that it was "one of the fleetest Race mares in the West."

4. *The Devil Knows How to Ride,* Edward E. Leslie.

5. *Quantrill and the Border Wars,* William Elsey Connelley.

Chapter 11

1. Official Records of the War of the Rebellion, Series 1, Volume 41, Part 1, pp. 440-441.

2. *The Devil Knows How to Ride,* Edward E. Leslie.

Chapter 12

1. *Brush Men and Vigilantes,* David Pickering and Judy Falls, Texas A&M Press, 2000.

2. *When the Yankee Soldiers Made a Run for Safety,* Captain J. E. Carraway, Lucas Papers, Sherman, Texas, Public Library.

Epilogue

1. *Quantrill and His Civil War Guerrillas,* Carl W. Breihan, Promontory Press, 1959.

2. Official Records of the War of the Rebellion, Series 1, Volume 41, Part 1, p. 442.

3. Official Records of the War of the Rebellion, Series 1, Volume 48, Part 2, pp. 705-706.

4. *Younger Brothers,* Carl W. Breihan, The Naylor Company, 1961.

5. Ibid.

6. Paw Paw regiments were made up of Southern soldiers and sympathizers who had taken the oath of allegiance.

7. *John Edwards Life, Writings and Tributes,* Kansas City, 1889, p. 233.

8. *The Devil Knows How to Ride,* Edward E. Leslie, Da Capo Press, 1996.

9. *Mistress of Glen Eden,* Sherrie S. McLeRoy.

10. *Confederate Military History,* Col. O. M. Roberts, Confederate Publishing Co., Atlanta, Georgia, 1899.

11. *Mistress of Glen Eden,* Sherrie S. McLeRoy.

Appendix II

1. *Quantrill and the Border Wars,* John Elsey Connelley.

BIBLIOGRAPHY

Breihan, Carl W. *Life and Times of Jesse James,* Frederick Fell, Inc., 1953.
———. *Quantrill and His Civil War Guerrillas,* Promontory Press, 1959.
———. *Sam Hildebrand, Guerrilla,* Leather Stocking Books, 1984.
———. *Younger Brothers,* The Naylor Company, 1961.
Boatner, Mark, III. *Civil War Dictionary,* David McKay Co., 1959.
Boswell, E. M. "Rebel Religion," *Civil War Times Illustrated,* October 1972.
Bourland Family Papers. Sherman, Texas Public Library.
Britton, Morris L. "Colbert's Ferry," *Chronicles of Oklahoma,* summer 1979.
Britton, Wiley. *Memoirs of the Rebellion on the Border, 1863,* University of Nebraska Press, 1993.
Brownlee, Richard S. *Gray Ghosts of the Confederacy: Guerilla Warfare in the West, 1861–1865,* Louisiana State Press, 1958.
Burch, J. P. *A True Story of Chas. W. Quantrell and His Guerila Band,* as told to Captain Harrison Trow, 1923.
Castel, Albert. *William Clarke Quantrill: His Life and Times,* Frederick Fell, 1962.
———, and Thomas Goodrich. *Bloody Bill Anderson: The Short, Savage Life of a Civil War Guerrilla,* Stackpole Books, 1998.
Carraway, Captain J. E. *When the Yankee Soldiers Made a Run for Safety,* The McCuistion Collection, "Loose Leaves of the History of Lamar County."
Carter, Forrest. *Gone to Texas,* University of New Mexico Press, 1976.
Connelley, William Elsey. *Quantrill and the Border Wars,* The Torch Press, 1910.
Dallas Morning News, Death of Allen Palmer, September 26, 1923
Duke, Betty Dorsett. *Jesse James Lived and Died in Texas,* Eakin Press, 1998.
Dyer, Robert L. *Jesse James and the Civil War in Missouri,* University of Missouri Press, 1994.
Eakin, Joanne, and Donald Hall, compilers. *Branded as Rebels,* Lucas Papers, Sherman, Texas, Public Library, 1993.
Edwards, John. *Noted Guerrillas and the Warfare on the Border,* 1877.
Faust, Patricia, editor. *Encyclopedia of the Civil War,* Harper and Row, 1986.
Fehrenbach, T. R. *Lone Star: A History of Texas and the Texans,* American Legacy Press, 1983.

Fellman, Michael. *Inside War: The Guerrilla Conflict in Missouri During the American Civil War,* Oxford University Press, 1959.

Fremantle, Arthur James Lyon. *The Fremantle Diary,* Little, Brown and Company, 1954.

Fyfer, J. Thomas. *History of Boone County,* Western Historical Society, 1882.

Gallaway, B. P., editor. *Texas: The Dark Corner of the Confederacy: Contemporary Accounts of the Lone Star State in the Civil War,* University of Nebraska Press, Third Edition, 1994.

Goodrich, Thomas. *Black Flag: Guerilla Warfare on the Western Border, 1861-1865,* Indiana University Press, 1995.

———. *Bloody Dawn: The Story of the Lawrence Massacre,* Kent State University Press, 1991.

Grayson County Marriage Records, Vol. B-1, Page 213. Marriage certificate of Bill Anderson and Bush Smith.

Gregg, William H. *A Little Dab of History Without Embellishment,* The Western Historical Manuscript Collection, University of Missouri.

Landom and Smith. *Grayson County Illustrated History,* Historical Publishers, 1967.

Lathrop, Barnes. *Migration into East Texas, 1835–1860: A Study from the United States Census,* Texas State Historical Association, 1949.

Leslie, Edward E. *The Devil Knows How to Ride,* Da Capo Press, 1996.

Lucas and Hall. *History of Grayson County,* Scruggs Printing Co., 1936.

Long, E. B. *The Civil War Day by Day: An Almanac, 1861–1865,* Doubleday Publishers, 1971.

McCaslin, Richard B. *Tainted Breeze: The Great Hanging at Gainesville, Texas, 1862,* Louisiana State University Press, 1994.

McCorkle, John (written by O. S. Barton). *Three Years with Quantrill: A True Story, Told by His Scout, John McCorkle,* University of Oklahoma Press, reprint, 1992.

McLeRoy, Sherrie. *Black Land, Red River: A Pictorial History of Grayson County, Texas,* Donning Co. Publisher, 1993.

———. *Mistress of Glen Eden: The Life and Times of Texas Pioneer Sophia Porter* (Booklet), 1990

———. *Red River Women,* Republic of Texas Press, 1996.

Mendenhall, Williard Hall. *Missouri Ordeal, 1862-1864.* Diaries of Williard Hall Mendenhall, transcribed by Margaret Mendenhall Frazier, St. Martin's Press.

Monaghan, Jay. *Civil War on the Western Border 1854–1865,* University of Nebraska Press, 1993.

Murdock, Gene P. *Sam Hildebrand's Footprints: The Story of Major Samuel S. Hildebrand, Bushwacker,* Murdock's Historical Publications, 2000.

Neville, A. W. *The Red River Valley, Then and Now.* North Texas Publishing Company, 1948.

New York Herald, July 26, 1862.

New York Times, October 11, 1863.

Nunn, W. C. *Texas Under the Carpet Baggers.* University of Texas Press, 1962.

Oates, Stephen B. *Confederate Cavalry West of the River,* University of Texas Press, 1961.

Pakula, Marvin H. *Centennial Album of the Civil War,* Castle, 1960.

Pickering, David, and Judy Falls. *Brush Men and Vigilantes: Civil War Dissent in Texas,* Texas A&M University Press, 2000.

Ramsdell, Charles. *Reconstruction in Texas,* Peter Smith, 1910.

Rankin, Melinda. *Texas in 1850,* Texian Press, 1966.

Ray, Bright. *Legends of the Red River Valley,* The Naylor Company, 1941.

Roberts, Col. O. M. *Confederate Military History XI,* Confederate Publishing Co., Atlanta, Georgia, 1899.

Simpson, Harold B. *Texas in the War, 1861–1865,* Hill Junior College Press, 1965.

Steele, Mrs. J. M. *Quantrill's Letter to a Texas Woman,* in the *Sherman Democrat,* The Lucas Papers, Sherman Public Library, undated.

Suderow, Bryce A. *Thunder in Arcadia Valley: Price's Defeat, September 27, 1864.* Center of Regional History and Cultural Heritage, Southwest Missouri State University, Cape Girardeau, Missouri, 1986.

Texas Civil War Centennial Commission. *Texas in the Civil War: A Resume History,* 1962.

Thompson, Henry C. *Sam Hildebrand Rides Again,* Walsworth Publishing Company, 1992.

Timmons, Joe T. *Texas on the Road to Secession II,* Doctor of Philosophy Dissertation, Chicago, 1973.

Triplett, Frank, comp. The *Life, Times, and Treacherous Death of Jesse James,* Swallow Press, 1970.

Wright, Marcus J., comp. *Texas in the War, 1861–1865,* Hill County College Press, 1965.

INDEX

ABOUT THE AUTHOR

Evault Boswell was born in 1928 at Framington, Missouri. He and his wife Jackie (McDaniel) Boswell have three grown children, eight grandchildren, two great-grandsons, and two great-granddaughters. They have been married for fifty-four years.

He graduated from Farmington, Missouri, High School in 1946 and attended Flat River, Missouri, Junior College.

He spent eighteen years in the retail business, moving to Greenville, Texas, in 1959 as manager of the F. W. Woolworth Store. He spent fifteen years in real estate and home construction in Greenville and for seventeen years managed Zephyr Baptist Encampment near Corpus Christi, Texas. He has also worked as the sports editor of the *Greenville-Herald Banner* and currently writes a column on birding for two Texas papers.

He has also written three manuals on camp management, which are in use by church camps across the country.

Boswell has made presentations to many genealogical and historical societies and at many Sons of Confederate Veterans meetings. He has also spoken about the Civil War at various service clubs and schools.

Writing credits include: *Civil War Times*, *Reader's Digest*, *Texas Star Magazine*, *Journal of Christian Camping*, *Alive*, and numerous other publications.

Texas Boys in Gray, published by the Republic of Texas Press, was his first nonfiction book and was released in 2000. The book is based on testimonies of the men who fought for the South and on the book published in 1912 by Mamie Yeary, *Reminiscences of the Boys in Gray*.

Birding Texas with Children was published by Republic of Texas Press in 2001. It is a travel guide to family-friendly birding sites in Texas.

The Rebel from Shepherd Mountain is a historical novel based on the biography of Sam Hildebrand, the noted bushwhacker from St. Francois County, Missouri. The story follows the real-life adventures of Sam as he hunts down and kills his personal enemies and declares war on the Union. The fictional character is a teenager whose father was killed by Federal soldiers. Aaron Bloom joins Sam, and their lives become entwined as Aaron seeks to revenge his father's death and finds love and the meaning of life.

Retirement Is for the Birds is a collection of columns on birding written over the past seven years that ran in the *Greenville Herald-Banner* and the *Brazosport Facts*. The columns were written to appeal to both the avid birder and the back-yard birder. Mostly humorous, with an emphasis on convervation, the stories include most the more popular birding areas in Texas. Fall 2003 publication.

www.ingramcontent.com/pod-product-compliance
Lightning Source LLC
Chambersburg PA
CBHW021400090426
42742CB00009B/930